JUNIOR GREAT BOOKS®

Nonfiction Inquiry 3

Student Log

This log belongs to:

The Great Books Foundation
A nonprofit educational organization

All articles © 2015 The Great Books Foundation.

Junior Great Books® is a registered trademark of the Great Books Foundation.

Shared Inquiry™ is a trademark of the Great Books Foundation.

The contents of this publication include proprietary trademarks
and copyrighted materials and may be used or quoted only with
permission and appropriate credit to the Foundation.

Copyright © 2015 by The Great Books Foundation

Chicago, Illinois

All rights reserved

ISBN 978-1-939014-37-5

First Printing

2 4 6 8 9 7 5 3 1

Printed in the United States of America

Published and distributed by

THE GREAT BOOKS FOUNDATION
A nonprofit educational organization

35 East Wacker Drive, Suite 400

Chicago, IL 60601

www.greatbooks.org

CONTENTS

Introduction 1

UNIT 1
Can Robots Be People Too? 7

UNIT 2
Small Acts Make a Big Difference 21

UNIT 3
Becoming Francisco X. Alarcón 35

UNIT 4
Egg-cellent Bird Parents 49

UNIT 5
Weather Watchers 63

UNIT 6
Don't Swallow That Spider! 77

UNIT 7
Children of the Oregon Trail   91

UNIT 8
Grunts, Flops, and Dives!   105

UNIT 9
Burger with a Side of Shoe Polish   119

Writer's Checklist   131

INTRODUCTION

Welcome to Junior Great Books Nonfiction Inquiry! Most of us read nonfiction every day. We look up information online and read articles. We may follow instructions to put things together. But do we stop to think about what it means? Or how it connects to the world around us? In this program, you'll read nonfiction texts about important topics. Some texts will be about the past, and some about the present. You and your class will ask questions and think about what you've read. Then you will share your ideas about the text in a discussion.

How Shared Inquiry Works

You will start by reading a nonfiction text and writing questions about it. Any question you have is worth asking. Then you will all share these questions aloud. Some will be answered right away. Others will be saved for later.

Next, you will reread the text. This time you will mark places that help you answer the *focus question*. You will discuss this question as a class.

Shared Inquiry Discussion

A focus question always has more than one good answer. In Shared Inquiry™ discussion, you will give an answer to the question and back it up with evidence. That evidence will come from the text. It can also come from your knowledge and experiences. Even when you use your own knowledge as evidence, you need to explain how it supports your answer. The goal of discussion is not to find a right answer. It is to explore different answers together!

Your teacher will ask more questions during the discussion to help everyone think more deeply and give evidence. You and your classmates will listen to each other's ideas and tell what you think about them. The new ideas you hear may lead you to change or add to your first answer to the focus question.

When the discussion is over, people may have different answers. But everyone will have evidence for those answers and will understand the text better.

You may still have questions and thoughts about the text after you finish the discussion. See if you can track down some answers! To help you, your teacher might ask you to write about or research a topic that interests you.

Every time you practice Shared Inquiry activities like asking questions, rereading, and discussion, you become a stronger reader and thinker.

Shared Inquiry Discussion Guidelines

Following these guidelines in Shared Inquiry discussion will help everyone share ideas and learn from one another.

1. Read the text twice before the discussion.

2. Focus on discussing the text that everyone has read.

3. Support your ideas with evidence from the text, your knowledge about the topic, and your experiences.

4. Listen to other people's ideas. You may agree or disagree with someone's answer, or ask a question about it.

5. Expect the teacher to only ask questions.

Introduction 5

CAN ROBOTS BE PEOPLE TOO?

Prereading

In this unit, you'll read about robots that are being invented to help older people. Before you read, answer the questions below.

What Do You Know?

What do you already know about the way people use robots in real life?

_____
_____
_____
_____

What Do You Think?

Would you like to have a robot friend to talk to or get help from?

_____
_____
_____
_____

Each time you read the text, return to what you wrote here to see if new information changes or adds to your answers.

CHECK YOUR PROGRESS
After you finish this page, check the box above and go to the next page.

Unit 1

First Reading 1 — Instructions

1. As you read, mark a **?** wherever you are **confused or curious** about something.
2. After reading, look at the places you marked. Write your questions on sticky notes.
3. Choose two questions to bring to the sharing questions activity:
   - A question about a part that **confuses you the most**.
   - A question about a part that **interests you the most**.

Can Robots Be People Too?

Mary Klein

The highlighted words will be important to know as you work on this unit.

Would your grandma or grandpa like having a robot friend? They may soon get to see! Scientists in many countries are inventing robots to help care for the growing number of **seniors** in the world.

People today live longer than they used to. There are going to be lots more people over the age of 65 in the future. And that's a challenge.

Many seniors can't move easily. Cooking, bathing, and even getting up from a chair can be hard. Plus, older people sometimes feel lonely and need **companionship**. Family members often don't live close by or don't have

seniors: older people
companionship: friendship

enough time to help out. That means the need for caregivers will soon be much greater.

But taking care of seniors is hard work. It also doesn't pay well. **Experts** say there will be a **gap** between the number of people who want to *be* caregivers and the number of people who *need* caregivers. What will we do?

At Your Service

"Robots will start to fill in those gaps," says Jim Osborn. He is a scientist who builds robots. And it's not a question of when robot helpers will be coming. They're already here!

Some robots can help with simple, everyday tasks. Nursing robots can lift and move patients

---

experts: people who have special knowledge or skill in something

gap: a difference between two things

For a test, HERB tries to split apart an Oreo without breaking it.

or bring them breakfast in bed. A robot with 24 fingers washes hair and gives head rubs.

HERB stands for Home Exploring Robot Butler. HERB can open cabinets, carry cups, and take out the trash!

Other robots can **monitor** a person's health. GiraffPlus checks blood pressure and blood sugar levels. Doctors and family members can use the video screen to check in. A robot named Hector reminds patients to take their medicine. Hector also helps people if they fall. It can even hold onto their glasses so they don't lose them.

Robots like these can make it easier for older people to stay in their own homes.

monitor: to watch or check on something

Many people do not want to move into **care facilities**. And if robots can help with chores, human caregivers have more time to give companionship and personal care.

A 24-hour Friend?

But what happens when humans are not around? Scientists have also made social companion robots to provide both company and care.

Paro is soft, furry, and looks like a baby harp seal. Its job is to help older people in care facilities feel calmer and happier. When people pet and talk to Paro, it acts real. It can make noises, move its tail, and even blink its eyes. "Paro is my friend," said Kazuo Nashimura, who lives in a Japanese care facility. "I like it that he seems to understand human feelings."

Paro is a popular companionship robot in Japan.

care facilities: places that give care to people who need help taking care of themselves, such as seniors

Molly the robot talks when she hears her name. Molly can remind seniors about medicine and doctor visits. She can also suggest exercises, healthy foods, and fun things to do. Molly wears a touch screen computer with memory games. Doctors and family can use the computer screen and camera to visit.

Palro is about 16 inches tall, and has a head, two arms, and two legs. Palro can play games, have simple conversations, and lead exercises. "I was surprised because the robot's movements were just like a human's," said one 69-year-old woman.

Molly

Thumbs Up or Thumbs Down?

"I really expect there will be a robot helping me out when I retire," says Jim Osborn.

But not all health workers, scientists, or older people think robots are a good idea. Robotics expert Noel Sharkey agrees that robots can help older people live by themselves. But he worries that people could be "left in the hands of machines." Then their human caregivers might not check on them as much.

Palro

Edith Garside is 90 years old. She accepts some **technology**, like the **panic button** she wears. But she says she would hate having a robot caregiver. She wants her caregivers to be human.

Sherry Turkle is an expert in social robots. She agrees that robots are no substitute for real people. She felt sad when she saw a woman talking to Paro. Turkle said the conversation had "no meaning" because robots don't understand feelings.

Men and women at a Japanese care facility exercise with Palro.

But talking to a robot might still be better than being alone. Turkle said the woman "found comfort when she **confided** in her Paro."

Other people point out that **interacting** with a robot is like using computers and smartphones. We use these **devices** every day and can get attached to them. Professor Wendy A. Rogers gives the example of your

---

technology: machines or pieces of equipment created to be useful or to solve problems
panic button: a device you can use to call someone for help
confided: told someone secret or private things
interacting: talking or doing things with others
devices: machines or tools that are created for a special purpose

Unit 1   13

car's **GPS**. "You talk to it and it talks to you. This isn't a bad thing. It's just what we do," she said.

Louise Aronson is a professor of **geriatrics**. She thinks that "the biggest argument for robot caregivers is that we need them." But does needing more caregivers make it okay to use robots? Will your grandparents want to chat with a robot instead of a person? Will *you*?

GPS: short for Global Positioning System, a device that uses satellite signals to tell you where you are and give directions to other places

geriatrics: an area of medicine that deals with old age

Quotes in text from:
- "Disruptions: Helper Robots Are Steered, Tentatively, to Care for the Aging," *New York Times*.
- "'A Robot is My Friend': Can Machines Care for the Elderly?" *BBC News*.
- "Next 10 Years Crucial for Japan's Nursing-Care Robot Industry," *Nikkei Asian Review*.
- "The Future of Robot Caregivers," *New York Times*.
- "Can Technology Fill the Elderly Care Gap?" *Telegraph*.

First Reading 1

CHECK YOUR PROGRESS

After you mark the text with **?**s, write your questions and choose two of them to bring to the sharing questions activity. Then check the box above and go to the next page.

CAN ROBOTS BE PEOPLE TOO?

Check Your Understanding — Instructions

- Read each question and the answer choices carefully.
- Look back at the text to answer the question.
- Fill in the circle next to the answer you choose.
- After you finish the quiz, turn to the next page.

1. Which of these is a main reason why scientists are inventing robots for seniors?
    - Ⓐ People will use more technology in the future.
    - Ⓑ A growing number of seniors will need care in the future.
    - Ⓒ People need more friends to talk to as they grow older.
    - Ⓓ Robots are better than humans at simple, everyday tasks.

2. Which activity would be best for a person who wants **companionship**?
    - Ⓐ calling a friend
    - Ⓑ taking a nap
    - Ⓒ planting a garden
    - Ⓓ reading a book

3. What is the main idea of the text?
    - Ⓐ Robots can understand the emotions of older people.
    - Ⓑ Robots can check blood pressure and sugar levels.
    - Ⓒ Robot caregivers may become more common in the future.
    - Ⓓ Not everyone has time to do all the things a robot can do.

4. Which detail from the text best supports your answer to question 3?
    - Ⓐ "'I like it that he seems to understand human feelings.'" (p. 11)
    - Ⓑ "Other robots can monitor a person's health." (p. 10)
    - Ⓒ "But taking care of seniors is hard work." (p. 9)
    - Ⓓ "'I really expect there will be a robot helping me out when I retire,' says Jim Osborn." (p. 12)

CAN ROBOTS BE PEOPLE TOO?

Second Reading

1. Reread "Can Robots Be People Too?" on pages 8–14. Mark a **G** where robots are **good** for taking care of older people. Mark a **B** where robots are **bad** for taking care of older people.

2. After you finish reading, look at the places you marked with a **G** and a **B**. Use what you marked to help you write an answer to this focus question:

   Do you think it is a good idea or a bad idea to use robots to help take care of older people?

   _____
   _____
   _____

3. Give two pieces of evidence to support your answer above.

   One piece of evidence that supports your answer:

   _____
   _____

   > Your evidence can be:
   > - A detail from the text, like a fact or a quote
   > - A detail from a photo, chart, or other text feature

   Another piece of evidence that supports your answer:

   _____
   _____

   > **CHECK YOUR PROGRESS** ☐
   > After you reread, make notes, and complete this page, check the box above. When it's time for the discussion, go to the next page.

16   Nonfiction Inquiry 3

CAN ROBOTS BE PEOPLE TOO?

Shared Inquiry Discussion

1 Use the answer and evidence you wrote on the previous page to participate in the Shared Inquiry discussion.

2 After discussion, think about whether your answer changed or stayed the same. Write it below. Then write a piece of evidence that changed or strengthened your answer.

Your answer to the focus question after discussion:

_____

_____

_____

_____

Evidence you found or that someone else used that helped you *(circle one)* **change your answer / make your first answer stronger:**

_____

_____

_____

_____

CHECK YOUR PROGRESS
After you finish this page, check the box above and go to the next page.

Unit 1   17

CAN ROBOTS BE PEOPLE TOO?

Essay Organizer

Write your answer to the essay question. Then write three pieces of evidence that support your answer.

Essay question: _____

_____

_____

Your answer:

Evidence #1:

Your evidence can be:
- A detail from the text, like a fact or a quote
- A detail from a photo, chart, or other text feature
- A fact about the topic, and where you learned it

How this evidence supports your answer:

CAN ROBOTS BE PEOPLE TOO?

Evidence #2:

How this evidence supports your answer:

Evidence #3:

How this evidence supports your answer:

> Use these notes to write your essay. Then use the Writer's Checklist on page 131 to make sure your draft is ready to turn in.

CAN ROBOTS BE PEOPLE TOO?

Further Investigation

1. Look at the questions you wrote on sticky notes and the class list of questions. Think about questions that came up during your discussion, too. Are there any you still want to know more about?

2. Write your questions below, along with some ideas about how you might get started if you wanted to answer them. (For instance, you might look for an answer online, read a book on the topic, or ask an expert.)

Questions you still want answered:	How you might find an answer:

SMALL ACTS MAKE A BIG DIFFERENCE

Prereading

In this unit, you'll read about three kids who came up with great ways to help people in their communities. Before you read, answer the questions below.

What Do You Know?

What does it mean to be part of a community?

_____

_____

_____

_____

What Do You Think?

What's one thing you could do to make your community a better place?

_____

_____

_____

_____

Each time you read the text, return to what you wrote here to see if new information changes or adds to your answers.

CHECK YOUR PROGRESS ☐

After you finish this page, check the box above and go to the next page.

First Reading 1: Instructions

1. As you read, mark a **?** wherever you are **confused or curious** about something.
2. After reading, look at the places you marked. Write your questions on sticky notes.
3. Choose two questions to bring to the sharing questions activity:
   - A question about a part that **confuses you the most**.
   - A question about a part that **interests you the most**.

Small Acts Make a Big Difference

Amanda Gebhardt

> The **highlighted words** will be important to know as you work on this unit.

Think about all the people who live in your community. How many of them do you know? How many are strangers? Even if you don't know everyone in your community, they are **connected** to you in some way. You live in the same place. You share the same surroundings. And sometimes things happen in your community that affect everyone.

This is why communities work together. Communities may hire crossing guards to keep students safe or set up gardens where people can grow vegetables and flowers. Communities may have people pick up litter along roads or have after-school sports programs for everyone.

---

connected: joined together

Volunteers clean up after Hurricane Sandy.

After big storms or earthquakes, communities come together to help rebuild homes and businesses.

Sometimes a single member of a community chooses to do something to make life better for others. Kids are no **exception**. Even something simple like sharing toys with a friend can make a community stronger. But kids can do much more than that.

Kymani Leads the Way

Kymani Quarrie is from Broward County, Florida. When he was seven, he saw people sleeping on the street. He asked his mom why they were there. She told him that they were homeless. Kymani

Kymani

---

exception: someone or something that is different from others

Unit 2   23

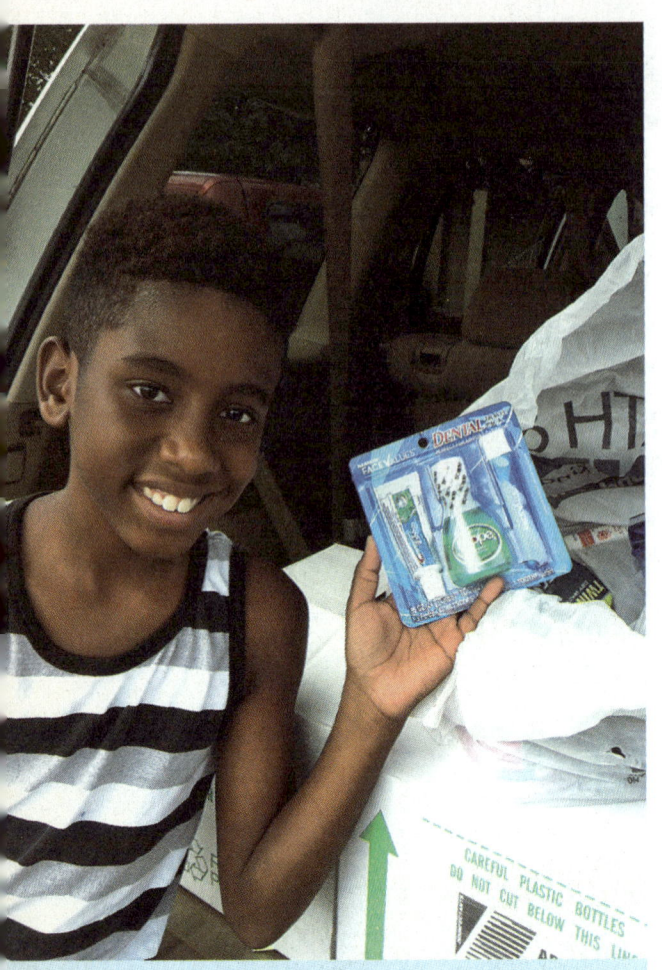

These are some of the items in Kymani's hygiene bags.

didn't think it was right that some people didn't have homes. He wanted to help.

Kymani's mom tried to find a homeless shelter where he could **volunteer**. But all the shelters said that Kymani was too young to help out. So, Kymani and his mom started their own group to raise money for homeless people called KQ Cares. After the first KQ Cares event, Kymani's group provided 500 meals to local homeless **residents**.

Twice a month, Kymani delivers 200 **hygiene** bags to homeless shelters. The bags contain everyday items that homeless people might not have, like soap and toothpaste. Since 2010, Kymani has led clothing drives, provided meals, and worked to make a better life for people in his community. No one can tell him he is too young to help now!

Abigail's Gift of Music

Abigail Lupi is from Stockholm, New Jersey. Abigail's great-grandmother lived in an **assisted living** center. When she was eight, Abigail

volunteer: to do work without getting paid for it
residents: people who live in a certain place
hygiene: things you do to keep yourself healthy
assisted living: housing and other services for people who need help taking care of themselves

sang there for her great-grandmother's 100th birthday. She saw how happy her singing made the other residents. "That's when I discovered many of the elderly didn't have visitors," Abigail recalled in an interview.

Abigail decided that she would be their visitor. She started to sing **regularly** for them. She invited some of her friends to join her. Before long, there were 15 girls from ages six to thirteen singing together! They sang at assisted living centers, nursing homes, and children's hospitals all over New Jersey.

Abigail and her friends named themselves the CareGirlz. They learned more than 90 songs, from pop hits to Broadway show tunes. Abigail is **dedicated** to making sure the people in her community don't feel lonely. "I like to brighten up people's days and help them have a fun time," she said. "If I do my best, they'll have a smile on their faces by the end."

---

regularly: very often
dedicated: completely focused on a certain task or goal

Unit 2   25

Jessica's Care Bears

Jessica Carscadden wanted to help people smile, too. She was born in China. She spent the first five years of her life in an orphanage. Her life changed when she was adopted by a family in San Diego. But change can be scary, even if it's a good change. Jessica's stuffed animals **comforted** her. They helped her feel less afraid.

Jessica wanted to share that feeling. So she **donated** all of her stuffed animals to the local fire department to comfort kids rescued from fires. Jessica knew that firefighters and police officers helped a lot of scared kids. Jessica wanted to make sure that every scared kid felt safe and loved. So she started a project called We Care Bears.

---

comforted: made someone feel less scared or upset
donated: gave money or things to help people or groups

Jessica and her family asked others to help. For their first project, they collected over 3,000 stuffed bears. They filled about 580 bags. Because of We Care Bears, every police car and fire engine in San Diego had stuffed animals ready for any kid who needed comfort.

We Care Bears has grown since Jessica started it. Now, three other states have stuffed animals from We Care Bears in police cars, too.

Jessica and some of her donated stuffed animals.

Choose to Make a Change!

Kymani, Abigail, and Jessica realized they had the power to make positive changes in people's lives. Each day, communities grow stronger because of kids like them.

Young volunteers help the victims of Hurricane Sandy in Staten Island, New York.

Quotes from Abigail Lupi from "8 Amazing Kids Who Make a Difference," *Parenting*.

Think back to the people in your community. What do you know about the needs of the people around you? What could you do to make a difference? Whatever you decide, start making that change! Even a small step can make a big difference. The future depends on what you and other young people choose to do.

First Reading 1

CHECK YOUR PROGRESS

After you mark the text with ?s, write your questions and choose two of them to bring to the sharing questions activity. Then check the box above and go to the next page.

SMALL ACTS MAKE A BIG DIFFERENCE

Check Your Understanding — Instructions

- Read each question and the answer choices carefully.
- Look back at the text to answer the question.
- Fill in the circle next to the answer you choose.
- After you finish the quiz, turn to the next page.

1. What does the text say is always true about all communities?
   - Ⓐ The people in a community are strangers.
   - Ⓑ The people in a community know each other.
   - Ⓒ The people in a community are connected in some way.
   - Ⓓ The people in a community live on the same street.

2. Which of these is a **resident** of your community?
   - Ⓐ a homeless shelter
   - Ⓑ your neighbor
   - Ⓒ your school
   - Ⓓ the fire department

3. What is the main idea of the text?
   - Ⓐ Most kids do more for their communities than adults.
   - Ⓑ Kids can find ways to make their communities better.
   - Ⓒ Most kids know only some people in their communities.
   - Ⓓ Kids wonder why people in their communities are homeless.

4. Which detail from the text best supports your answer to question 3?
   - Ⓐ "So, Kymani and his mom started their own group to raise money for homeless people called KQ Cares." (p. 24)
   - Ⓑ "When he was seven, he saw people sleeping on the street." (p. 23)
   - Ⓒ "And sometimes things happen in your community that affect everyone." (p. 22)
   - Ⓓ "This is why communities work together." (p. 22)

SMALL ACTS MAKE A BIG DIFFERENCE

Second Reading 2

1. Reread "Small Acts Make a Big Difference" on pages 22–28. Mark an **H** where you read about something you think would **help** your own community.

2. After you finish reading, look at the places you marked with an **H**. Use what you marked to help you write an answer to this focus question:

   Which of these ways to help your community would you most want to try?

   _____

   _____

   _____

3. Give two pieces of evidence to support your answer above.

   One piece of evidence that supports your answer:

   _____

   _____

   _____

   > **Your evidence can be:**
   > - A detail from the text, like a fact or a quote
   > - A detail from a photo, chart, or other text feature

   Another piece of evidence that supports your answer:

   _____

   _____

   _____

   > **CHECK YOUR PROGRESS** ☐
   > After you reread, make notes, and complete this page, check the box above. When it's time for the discussion, go to the next page.

30 Nonfiction Inquiry 3

SMALL ACTS MAKE A BIG DIFFERENCE

Shared Inquiry Discussion

1 Use the answer and evidence you wrote on the previous page to participate in the Shared Inquiry discussion.

2 After discussion, think about whether your answer changed or stayed the same. Write it below. Then write a piece of evidence that changed or strengthened your answer.

Your answer to the focus question after discussion:

_____
_____
_____
_____

Evidence you found or that someone else used that helped you *(circle one)* **change your answer / make your first answer stronger:**

_____
_____
_____
_____

CHECK YOUR PROGRESS
After you finish this page, check the box above and go to the next page.

Unit 2   31

SMALL ACTS MAKE A BIG DIFFERENCE

Essay Organizer

Write your answer to the essay question. Then write three pieces of evidence that support your answer.

Essay question: _____

_____

_____

Your answer:

Evidence #1:

How this evidence supports your answer:

Your evidence can be:
- A detail from the text, like a fact or a quote
- A detail from a photo, chart, or other text feature
- A fact about the topic, and where you learned it

32   Nonfiction Inquiry 3

SMALL ACTS MAKE A BIG DIFFERENCE

Evidence #2:

How this evidence supports your answer:

Evidence #3:

How this evidence supports your answer:

> Use these notes to write your essay. Then use the Writer's Checklist on page 131 to make sure your draft is ready to turn in.

SMALL ACTS MAKE A BIG DIFFERENCE

Further Investigation

1. Look at the questions you wrote on sticky notes and the class list of questions. Think about questions that came up during your discussion, too. Are there any you still want to know more about?

2. Write your questions below, along with some ideas about how you might get started if you wanted to answer them. (For instance, you might look for an answer online, read a book on the topic, or ask an expert.)

Questions you still want answered:	How you might find an answer:

BECOMING FRANCISCO X. ALARCÓN

Prereading

In this unit, you'll read about the poet Francisco X. Alarcón and how he became the person he is today. Before you read, answer the questions below.

What Do You Know?

What is something that has happened in your life that is very important to you? Why was it important?

_____

_____

_____

_____

What Do You Think?

Why do you think some writers write stories and poems about their own lives?

_____

_____

_____

_____

Each time you read the text, return to what you wrote here to see if new information changes or adds to your answers.

CHECK YOUR PROGRESS ☐

After you finish this page, check the box above and go to the next page.

Unit 3   35

First Reading 1: Instructions

1. As you read, mark a **?** wherever you are **confused or curious** about something.
2. After reading, look at the places you marked. Write your questions on sticky notes.
3. Choose two questions to bring to the sharing questions activity:
   - A question about a part that **confuses you the most**.
   - A question about a part that **interests you the most**.

Becoming Francisco X. Alarcón

Joyce McGreevy

> The **highlighted words** will be important to know as you work on this unit.

A collection of poetry is "like a tomato plant." So says poet Francisco X. Alarcón. "From a small seed it sprouts, then grows and grows. Poems need good soil, sunlight, water, air, and lots of care and **tending**," he adds.

Alarcón has written collections of poetry for young people and adults. Through his poetry, he **expresses** his **identity**. Most of his poems are published in Spanish, his first language, and also in English. "I write about life, about what happens to me, what happens to my friends, what happens to my family, what happens in

tending: caring for
expresses: says what a person thinks or feels, using words or gestures
identity: the things that make you who you are

the world," he says. The seeds for writing such personal poetry were planted in Alarcón at a young age.

Two Cultures

Alarcón was born in Wilmington, California in 1954. His mother's family left Mexico in 1917 and she was born in the United States. But after she married Alarcón's father, they often visited family in Mexico. Alarcón wrote about his memories of those trips in his poem "1. From the Bellybutton of the Moon/Del ombligo de la luna."

Here's how the poem begins:

1. From the Bellybutton of the Moon/ Del ombligo de la luna

cuando	whenever
digo	I say
"México"	"Mexico"
siento	I feel
en la cara	the same wind
el mismo viento	on my face
que sentía	I felt when
al abrir	I would open
la ventanilla	the window
en mi primer	on my first
viaje al sur	trip south
en coche	by car

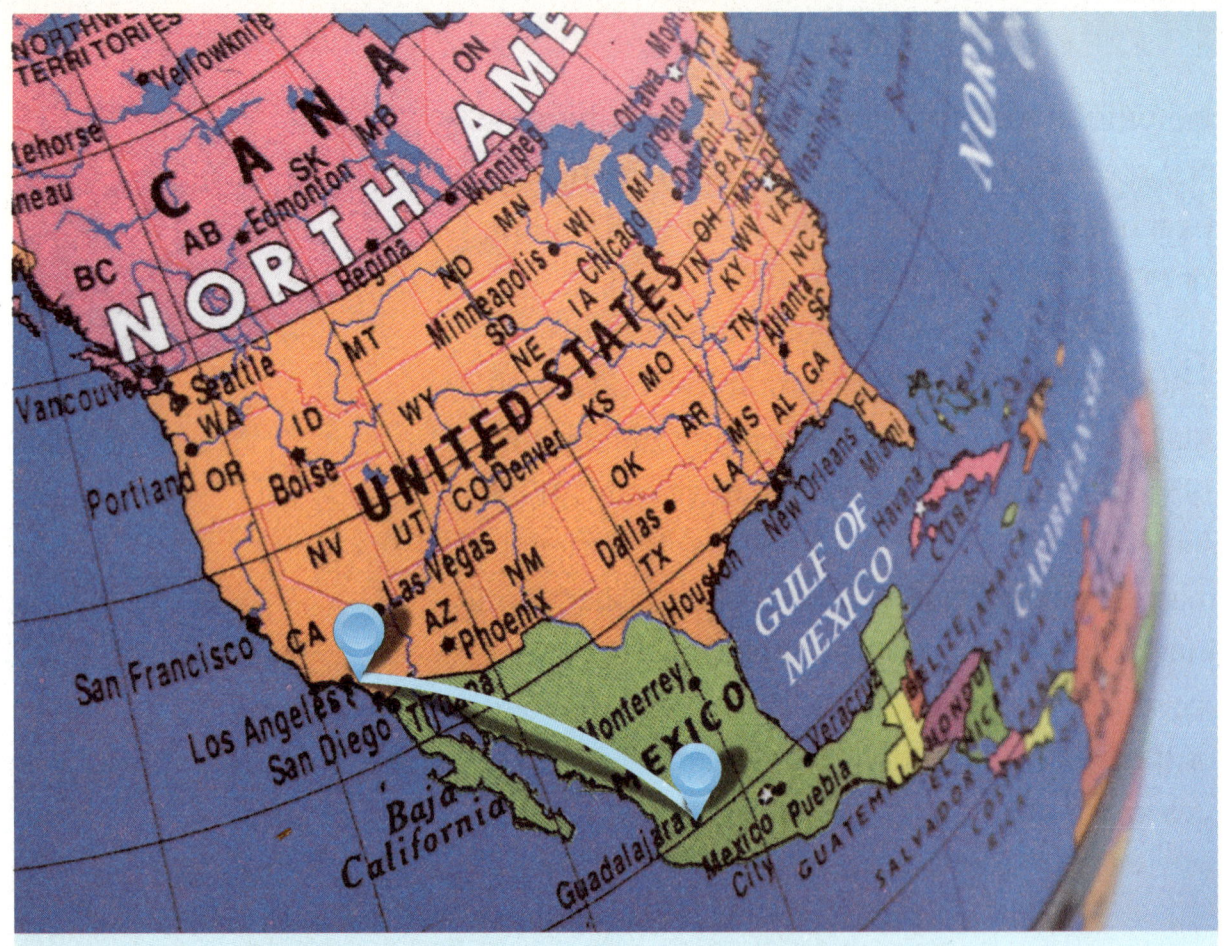

Alarcón moved from Wilmington, California to Guadalajara, Mexico when he was six.

Alarcón's family moved to Mexico when he was six. But when he was a young adult, Alarcón moved back to California. Because Alarcón has spent so much time in Mexico and the United States, he thinks of himself as **bicultural**.

Two Languages

Alarcón first began writing poetry as a teenager because of his *abuela* in Mexico. She sang

---

bicultural: belonging to two different cultures. Cultures are the beliefs and ways of life of a certain group of people.

abuela: Spanish for "grandmother"

beautiful songs. She created the songs herself, but she didn't write them down. Alarcón started to write them down for her. If he forgot a line, he would make up a new one.

He also loved his grandfather's tales of **ancient** Mexico. After Alarcón finished college, he studied in Mexico. There he wrote a book of poems in English, Spanish, and Nahuatl, the language of the Aztec people.

Being **bilingual** is important to Alarcón. "Imagine if I did not have **access** to the memories of my grandmother, or to my grandfather," he says in one interview. "If I could not talk to my uncles in Spanish, I would be very poor, as a person."

ancient: very old
bilingual: able to speak two languages
access: a way of being able to use something

Unit 3   39

Yes, You Can!

Alarcón wanted to become a poet from an early age. His father gave him a love of **literature**. "He was a reader of books all the time," Alarcón **recalls**. Alarcón says his mother was "the one who really pushed us" to succeed. She told her seven children, "Do whatever you want to do, but do it well!"

Alarcón and his brothers and sisters all went to college. The poem "My Mother's Hands/ Las manos de mi madre" tells how Alarcón's mother encouraged her children to do well in life.

Alarcón has written many books of poetry for children and adults.

literature: written works, like books, poems, and plays
recalls: remembers

Here is how the poem ends:

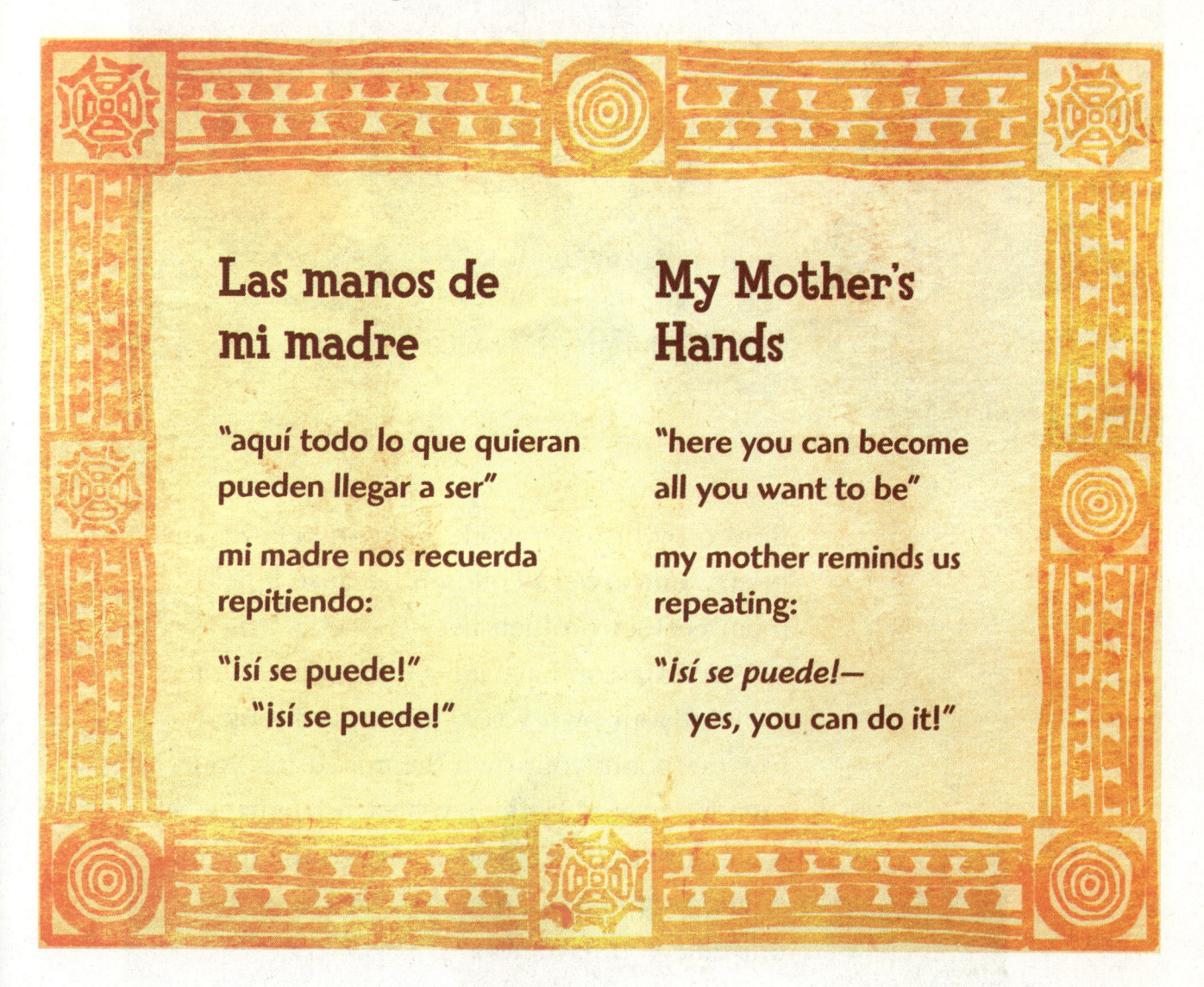

Las manos de mi madre

"aquí todo lo que quieran
pueden llegar a ser"

mi madre nos recuerda
repitiendo:

"¡sí se puede!"
    "¡sí se puede!"

My Mother's Hands

"here you can become
all you want to be"

my mother reminds us
repeating:

"*¡sí se puede!—*
    yes, you can do it!"

Find Your Voice

Alarcón likes to visit schools to talk about poetry with students. He suggests that students try writing about memories and family members. He says children can often do this "in no time, right there, on the spot."

Alarcón tells a story about one boy who wrote a poem. It began, "My father is tall and strong, and when he sees me, he laughs." When the boy read his poem aloud, he was very

Quotes in text from:
- *Laughing Tomatoes and Other Spring Poems*, Francisco X. Alarcón.
- "An Interview with Francisco X. Alarcón," colorincolorado.org.
- "Being Bilingual," Colorincolorado YouTube video.
- "Francisco Alarcón Interview," Leeandlow YouTube video.
- "Poetry Empowers," Colorincolorado YouTube video.
- "Poet Francisco Alarcón," Colorincolorado YouTube video.

moved by his own work. Alarcón believes that poetry **empowers** children because it helps them **reflect on** their lives.

Does Alarcón have advice for young writers?

"Find your own voice," he says. "It's okay to write about your own dreams, using your own language." He believes each language "is a window to the universe. And so the more windows you have, the more access to the universe you have, too."

empowers: gives someone the power to do something
reflect on: think carefully and deeply about

First Reading 1

CHECK YOUR PROGRESS

After you mark the text with ?s, write your questions and choose two of them to bring to the sharing questions activity. Then check the box above and go to the next page.

42   Nonfiction Inquiry 3

BECOMING FRANCISCO X. ALARCÓN

Check Your Understanding — Instructions

- Read each question and the answer choices carefully.
- Look back at the text to answer the question.
- Fill in the circle next to the answer you choose.
- After you finish the quiz, turn to the next page.

1. Which of these does Alarcón suggest students do when they write poetry?
   - Ⓐ He suggests they write about memories and family.
   - Ⓑ He suggests they use fancy words.
   - Ⓒ He suggests they use Spanish and English.
   - Ⓓ He suggests they write about traveling.

2. Which of these things can a **bilingual** person do?
   - Ⓐ live in two countries
   - Ⓑ speak two languages
   - Ⓒ go to college
   - Ⓓ write good poetry

3. What is the main idea of the text?
   - Ⓐ Alarcón's poetry is about the people and places that made him who he is.
   - Ⓑ Alarcón's poetry is about both Mexico and the United States.
   - Ⓒ Alarcón visits schools and talks to students about poetry.
   - Ⓓ Alarcón became a poet because he loved to read.

4. Which detail from the text supports your answer to question 3?
   - Ⓐ "His father gave him a love of literature." (p. 40)
   - Ⓑ "Alarcón's family moved to Mexico when he was six." (p. 38)
   - Ⓒ "Through his poetry, he expresses his identity." (p. 36)
   - Ⓓ "He believes each language 'is a window to the universe.'" (p. 42)

BECOMING FRANCISCO X. ALARCÓN

Second Reading 2

1. Go back and reread "Becoming Francisco X. Alarcón" on pages 36–42. As you read, mark an **I** where you read something about Francisco X. Alarcón's life that seems **important** to him.

2. After you finish reading, look at the places you marked with an **I**. Use what you marked to help you write an answer to this focus question:

   Why do you think Francisco X. Alarcón chooses to write poems about his life?

   _____

   _____

   _____

3. Give two pieces of evidence to support your answer above.

   One piece of evidence that supports your answer:

   _____

   _____

   Your evidence can be:
   - A detail from the text, like a fact or a quote
   - A detail from a photo, chart, or other text feature

   Another piece of evidence that supports your answer:

   _____

   _____

   CHECK YOUR PROGRESS
   After you reread, make notes, and complete this page, check the box above. When it's time for the discussion, go to the next page.

44 Nonfiction Inquiry 3

BECOMING FRANCISCO X. ALARCÓN

Shared Inquiry Discussion

1 Use the answer and evidence you wrote on the previous page to participate in the Shared Inquiry discussion.

2 After discussion, think about whether your answer changed or stayed the same. Write it below. Then write a piece of evidence that changed or strengthened your answer.

Your answer to the focus question after discussion:

_____
_____
_____
_____

Evidence you found or that someone else used that helped you *(circle one)* **change your answer / make your first answer stronger:**

_____
_____
_____
_____

CHECK YOUR PROGRESS
After you finish this page, check the box above and go to the next page.

Unit 3   45

BECOMING FRANCISCO X. ALARCÓN

Essay Organizer

Write your answer to the essay question. Then write three pieces of evidence that support your answer.

Essay question: _____

_____

_____

Your answer:

Evidence #1:

How this evidence supports your answer:

Your evidence can be:
- A detail from the text, like a fact or a quote
- A detail from a photo, chart, or other text feature
- A fact about the topic, and where you learned it

BECOMING FRANCISCO X. ALARCÓN

Evidence #2:

How this evidence supports your answer:

Evidence #3:

How this evidence supports your answer:

> Use these notes to write your essay. Then use the Writer's Checklist on page 131 to make sure your draft is ready to turn in.

BECOMING FRANCISCO X. ALARCÓN

Further Investigation

1. Look at the questions you wrote on sticky notes and the class list of questions. Think about questions that came up during your discussion, too. Are there any you still want to know more about?

2. Write your questions below, along with some ideas about how you might get started if you wanted to answer them. (For instance, you might look for an answer online, read a book on the topic, or ask an expert.)

Questions you still want answered:	How you might find an answer:

Nonfiction Inquiry 3

EGG-CELLENT BIRD PARENTS

Prereading In this unit, you'll read about the things bird parents do to protect their eggs and their babies. Before you read, answer the questions below.

What Do You Know?

What do you already know about how birds hatch their eggs?

_____

_____

_____

_____

What Do You Think?

What problems do you think a bird might face when trying to hatch its eggs?

_____

_____

_____

_____

Each time you read the text, return to what you wrote here to see if new information changes or adds to your answers.

CHECK YOUR PROGRESS
After you finish this page, check the box above and go to the next page.

Unit 4 49

First Reading 1: Instructions

1. As you read, mark a **?** wherever you are **confused or curious** about something.
2. After reading, look at the places you marked. Write your questions on sticky notes.
3. Choose two questions to bring to the sharing questions activity:
   - A question about a part that **confuses you the most**.
   - A question about a part that **interests you the most**.

Egg-cellent Bird Parents

Jennifer Kleiman

The highlighted words will be important to know as you work on this unit.

At one time, everyone was a baby. Your parents. Your teacher. Even your great-uncle Stan. They may act pretty smart and grown-up now. But they were once small, fussy, helpless blobs. They drooled. They cried. They needed an adult for everything!

It's a fact. Babies are terrible at taking care of themselves. None of us would have **survived** very long without someone to feed us and keep us warm and safe. Parents work hard to protect their babies. And it's not just human parents. Lots of animals do too.

Imagine you are a bird parent. Let's say you are a robin. You found a mate. You found the

survived: stayed alive

perfect spot to raise your babies. You are ready to begin **nesting**. First, you have to build a nest. You do this one beakful of grass at a time. Back and forth. Back and forth. Very slowly, you weave and shape your nest into a perfect cup. This **process** takes about two to six days.

Once you lay your eggs, you must keep them warm until they hatch. This means sitting on them quietly for two weeks straight, with only a few short breaks. Robins rarely leave their eggs for more than 5 to 10 minutes. How would you feel sitting in one place for two weeks? When the eggs finally hatch, you feed your featherless babies every 15 to 20 minutes *all day long*. That's a lot of bugs and worms.

But here's the most important part. You have to do all of this while making sure no one eats your babies. Bird eggs are a tasty meal to a lot of animals. So are baby birds. You think your parents had it hard? At least no one wanted to eat you when you were a baby!

nesting: building and living in a nest
process: a set of actions to make or do something

The robin gathers nesting material.

She weaves the nest into a cup.

The robin also uses mud to build her nest.

Unit 4   51

So what can a bird do to protect its eggs from hungry animals? First, birds make sure their nests are hard to spot. They often choose hidden places, like underneath leafy branches. Birds also choose nesting **materials** that match their **surroundings**. Scientists did a test with zebra finches to help prove this. They put the zebra finches in cages with colored walls. Then they gave the birds colorful strips of paper. For the most part, the finches built their nests with the strips that matched the color of their walls!

Zebra finch

Knock, Knock! Who's There? Mr. Hornbill.

Some birds hide their nests inside tree trunks. The great hornbill takes this one step further. First, the female hornbill builds her nest inside a large tree. Then the male uses mud and poop to seal up the hole in the tree with the female still inside. But don't worry! The male leaves a small hole so he can pass food to the female while she **incubates** the eggs. Once

The male hornbill feeds his family a few times a day.

---

materials: things needed to make or do something
surroundings: the place and the things around you
incubates: sits on eggs to keep them warm so they will hatch

the eggs hatch, the female stays with the chicks until they are almost ready to fly. Then she breaks out.

Killdeer: Total Fakers

Not all birds nest in trees. Some, like the killdeer, lay their eggs on the ground. This probably doesn't sound very safe. But these birds know what they're doing.

First, the male killdeer makes a shallow dent in the ground. Then he lines it with stones and sticks to help **camouflage** the eggs. The male makes a few of these nests. When he is finished, the female comes along to **inspect** his work. She chooses the nest she likes best to lay

A killdeer stands over its nest.

camouflage: to hide or change the look of something to make it hard to see
inspect: to look at very carefully

Unit 4 53

Even the killdeer chicks are hard to see!

her eggs in. Then both parents take turns incubating the eggs and caring for the chicks.

But wait. The eggs are still just lying on the ground. What if an animal finds them? Fear not! The killdeer has a plan. If anyone comes too close to the nest, it pretends to have a broken wing. The killdeer actually holds its wing out to one side to make it look broken. Then it cries like it's in pain, as it moves farther and farther from the nest. The **intruder** follows. An injured animal is an easy meal. Once the killdeer is a safe distance from the nest, it suddenly **recovers** and flies away. If there were an award for best bird actor, the killdeer would win.

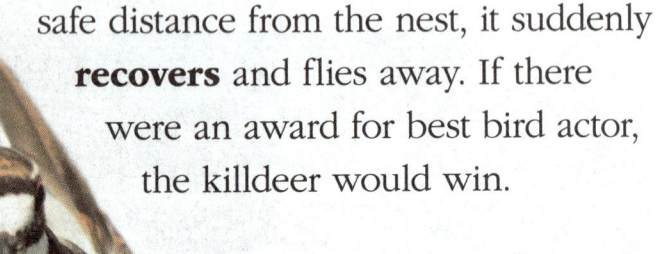

intruder: someone who enters a place without permission
recovers: feels well again after being sick or hurt

Cowbirds: Bullies of the Sky

Then there is the brown-headed cowbird. It doesn't even build a nest. This sneaky bird forces other birds to raise its babies. First, it finds a nest with eggs already in it. Then it destroys or removes one of the eggs and replaces it with one of its own eggs!

These sparrow chicks look tiny next to the cowbird chick at the bottom.

From time to time, the cowbird will return to check on its egg. If the owner of the nest has removed it, the cowbird gets very angry. She can get so angry that she might just destroy the nest or the eggs belonging to the other bird. What a bully!

Unit 4   55

An adult warbler feeds the much larger cowbird chick.

Birds have found some pretty clever ways to protect their eggs. Some are master builders. Others put on a big show. And then there are the cowbirds. They sure won't be getting any cards on Mother's Day. As far as they're concerned, parenting is **for the birds**!

for the birds: an expression that means "not worth it"

First Reading 1

CHECK YOUR PROGRESS

After you mark the text with ?s, write your questions and choose two of them to bring to the sharing questions activity. Then check the box above and go to the next page.

EGG-CELLENT BIRD PARENTS

Check Your Understanding — Instructions

- Read each question and the answer choices carefully.
- Look back at the text to answer the question.
- Fill in the circle next to the answer you choose.
- After you finish the quiz, turn to the next page.

1. Which of these things is something all the birds in this text do?
    - Ⓐ They make nests using grass.
    - Ⓑ They lay eggs inside trees.
    - Ⓒ They find ways to protect their eggs.
    - Ⓓ They hatch their eggs.

2. Which of these things does a bird do when it **incubates** its eggs?
    - Ⓐ It destroys the eggs.
    - Ⓑ It warms the eggs.
    - Ⓒ It hides the eggs.
    - Ⓓ It lays the eggs.

3. What is the main idea of the text?
    - Ⓐ Bird parents have different ways to keep their babies safe.
    - Ⓑ Bird parents build their nests in trees and on the ground.
    - Ⓒ Some bird parents pretend to be hurt to fool other animals.
    - Ⓓ Bird parents work hard to build perfect nests for their babies.

4. Which detail from the text best supports your answer to question 3?
    - Ⓐ "At one time, everyone was a baby." (p. 50)
    - Ⓑ "Bird eggs are a tasty meal to a lot of animals." (p. 51)
    - Ⓒ "Some are master builders." (p. 56)
    - Ⓓ "Parents work hard to protect their babies." (p. 50)

Unit 4

EGG-CELLENT BIRD PARENTS

Second Reading 2

1. Reread "Egg-cellent Bird Parents" on pages 50–56. Mark an **A** where you think a bird does something **amazing** to keep its eggs safe.

2. After you finish reading, look at the places you marked with an **A**. Use what you marked to help you write an answer to this focus question:

   Which do you think is the most amazing way to keep an egg safe?

   _____

   _____

   _____

3. Give two pieces of evidence to support your answer above.

   One piece of evidence that supports your answer:

   _____

   _____

   _____

   > Your evidence can be:
   > - A detail from the text, like a fact or a quote
   > - A detail from a photo, chart, or other text feature

   Another piece of evidence that supports your answer:

   _____

   _____

   _____

   > **CHECK YOUR PROGRESS** ☐
   > After you reread, make notes, and complete this page, check the box above. When it's time for the discussion, go to the next page.

58   Nonfiction Inquiry 3

EGG-CELLENT BIRD PARENTS

Shared Inquiry Discussion

1. Use the answer and evidence you wrote on the previous page to participate in the Shared Inquiry discussion.

2. After discussion, think about whether your answer changed or stayed the same. Write it below. Then write a piece of evidence that changed or strengthened your answer.

Your answer to the focus question after discussion:

_____

_____

_____

_____

Evidence you found or that someone else used that helped you *(circle one)* **change your answer / make your first answer stronger:**

_____

_____

_____

_____

CHECK YOUR PROGRESS
After you finish this page, check the box above and go to the next page.

EGG-CELLENT BIRD PARENTS

Essay Organizer

Write your answer to the essay question. Then write three pieces of evidence that support your answer.

Essay question: _____

_____

_____

Your answer:

Evidence #1:

How this evidence supports your answer:

Your evidence can be:
- A detail from the text, like a fact or a quote
- A detail from a photo, chart, or other text feature
- A fact about the topic, and where you learned it

EGG-CELLENT BIRD PARENTS

Evidence #2:

How this evidence supports your answer:

Evidence #3:

How this evidence supports your answer:

> Use these notes to write your essay. Then use the Writer's Checklist on page 131 to make sure your draft is ready to turn in.

EGG-CELLENT BIRD PARENTS

Further Investigation

1. Look at the questions you wrote on sticky notes and the class list of questions. Think about questions that came up during your discussion, too. Are there any you still want to know more about?

2. Write your questions below, along with some ideas about how you might get started if you wanted to answer them. (For instance, you might look for an answer online, read a book on the topic, or ask an expert.)

Questions you still want answered:	How you might find an answer:

WEATHER WATCHERS

Prereading

In this unit, you'll read about how we predict weather today and how people in the past watched animals to predict weather. Before you read, answer the questions below.

What Do You Know?

What are some ways that people find out what the weather will be like in the future?

_____
_____
_____
_____

What Do You Think?

Why do you think weather reports are sometimes wrong?

_____
_____
_____
_____

Each time you read the text, return to what you wrote here to see if new information changes or adds to your answers.

CHECK YOUR PROGRESS
After you finish this page, check the box above and go to the next page.

Unit 5

First Reading 1 — Instructions

1. As you read, mark a **?** wherever you are **confused or curious** about something.
2. After reading, look at the places you marked. Write your questions on sticky notes.
3. Choose two questions to bring to the sharing questions activity:
   - A question about a part that **confuses you the most**.
   - A question about a part that **interests you the most**.

Weather Watchers

Amanda Gebhardt

> The **highlighted words** will be important to know as you work on this unit.

Crack! Boom! Thunder and lightning fill the sky. Dark clouds roll in. Before you know it, it's pouring outside. Luckily, the weather **forecast** prepared you for this. You were safe inside long before a single raindrop had fallen.

Thanks to science, we often know what the weather will be before it even happens. Scientists who study weather conditions and make forecasts are called meteorologists.

Weather conditions include whether it will be calm or stormy. But they also include temperature, how wet or dry the air is, and how clear or cloudy the sky looks.

Meteorologists use special tools to gather information about the different weather

---

forecast: a statement about something that is likely to happen (especially weather)

The Storm Prediction Center watches for conditions that might produce tornadoes or strong thunderstorms.

conditions. For example, a tool called a barometer measures **air pressure**. Changes in air pressure can tell you if a storm is coming. Rising pressure means the weather will be fair. Falling pressure means a storm is on its way.

To make weather forecasts, meteorologists collect weather information and enter it into computers. The computers use math **formulas** to tell what the weather is going to be and how it might change based on past weather patterns. By studying these results, meteorologists can make **predictions** about future weather.

---

air pressure: the weight of air as it presses down on the earth
formulas: math rules that are shown in letters and numbers
predictions: statements about things that might happen in the future

A Guessing Game

Meteorologists know *a lot* about weather, but can they be sure about their predictions? The answer is no. Weather forecasts are really just educated guesses. The more days ahead you try to predict the weather, the less likely your forecast will be **accurate**.

But forecasts still give us a lot of useful information. They help us prepare for dangerous weather like hurricanes, tornadoes, and floods. Farmers also depend on forecasts to protect their crops from too much heat or cold.

Bird Barometers

Before meteorology, people looked for clues in nature to predict the weather. One thing people paid close attention to was animal **behavior**. For example, they noticed that animals often acted differently before a storm.

One way that people predicted storms was to pay attention to how high birds were flying in the sky. Birds flying high meant the weather would be calm. Birds flying low warned that a storm was on its way. Even today, we are not

---

accurate: correct
behavior: the way a person or animal acts

totally sure why birds act this way. But we have some good **theories**.

Have your ears ever popped from flying in a plane or traveling up a mountain? This is due to a change in air pressure.

Birds have a special organ in their ear called the Vitali organ. It can **detect** even the tiniest change in air pressure. Some scientists think that the change in air pressure before a storm might hurt a bird's ears when it is flying high. So when a storm is coming, birds fly low.

---

theories: ideas that are meant to explain certain facts or events
detect: to notice or discover

People in Ao Nang, Thailand, try to escape the 2004 tsunami.

The Sound of Danger

Changing air pressure isn't the only thing animals can sense. Earthquakes, hurricanes, and even high winds produce very low sounds, called infrasounds. They are too low for humans to hear, but some other animals can hear them. Elephants even use infrasound rumbles to talk to one another.

In 2004, a giant **tsunami** hit Indonesia. Before it hit, people reported seeing elephants running away from the beach. Bats were seen flying away from the area, and flocks of flamingos flew to higher ground. One man even reported that his dogs didn't want to go for their daily run on the beach. Infrasounds may have warned the animals the tsunami was coming.

tsunami: a giant ocean wave, usually caused by an underwater earthquake or volcano

Sharing Nature's Clues

Animal behavior can give us a lot of interesting clues about the weather. But some people argue that these **observations** have no place in modern weather science. In science, you need to be able to prove that something is true, and say why. But animals change their behavior for a lot of different reasons. There is no way to be completely sure that weather is the cause.

Still, people have been observing nature for a very long time. Long before we looked to technology for weather clues, we looked at the world. We noticed many things that science has not yet explained. To help remember and share these clues, people made up proverbs, or catchy sayings about what they believe.

Weather Proverbs

1. If the cat washes her face over her ear, the weather is sure to be fine and clear.
2. Cold is the night when stars shine bright.
3. Bees will not swarm before a storm.
4. If birds fly low, then rain we shall know.
5. The sudden storm lasts not three hours.
6. Birds on a telephone wire predict the coming of rain.
7. When leaves show their undersides, be very sure that rain **betides**.

observations: things you notice by watching
betides: happens

Unit 5 69

Watch, Look, and Listen

Only now are we beginning to understand the science behind some of these observations. Others may have little or no science behind them at all!

So what should we trust when we want to predict the weather? The first step to figuring it out is to do what scientists do. Observe!

All science begins with observation. Start by paying attention to what you see, hear, feel, and even smell. Watch your cat. Look at the stars. Sniff the air. Then record what you notice. Over time, you might begin to notice patterns. You might even discover new ways to predict the weather all on your own.

First Reading 1

CHECK YOUR PROGRESS

After you mark the text with ?s, write your questions and choose two of them to bring to the sharing questions activity. Then check the box above and go to the next page.

WEATHER WATCHERS

Check Your Understanding

Instructions

- Read each question and the answer choices carefully.
- Look back at the text to answer the question.
- Fill in the circle next to the answer you choose.
- After you finish the quiz, turn to the next page.

1. Which of these things may make birds fly low?
   - Ⓐ infrasound rumbles
   - Ⓑ changes in air pressure
   - Ⓒ changes in temperature
   - Ⓓ heavy rainfall

2. Which of these is an example of a weather **prediction**?
   - Ⓐ a meteorologist saying it is likely to rain
   - Ⓑ a person making up a proverb about storms
   - Ⓒ a scientist measuring the air pressure
   - Ⓓ a person looking up the temperature online

3. What is the main idea of the text?
   - Ⓐ Meteorologists use tools to figure out what the weather will be.
   - Ⓑ Forecasts can help people prepare for dangerous weather.
   - Ⓒ No one has found the perfect way to predict the weather.
   - Ⓓ Scientists have finally found the perfect way to predict weather.

4. Which detail from the text supports your answer to question 3?
   - Ⓐ "Weather forecasts are really just educated guesses." (p. 66)
   - Ⓑ "You were safe inside long before a single raindrop had fallen." (p. 64)
   - Ⓒ "You might even discover new ways to predict the weather all on your own." (p. 70)
   - Ⓓ "For example, a tool called a barometer measures air pressure." (p. 65)

WEATHER WATCHERS

Second Reading 2

1. Reread "Weather Watchers" on pages 64–70. Mark a **T** where meteorologists should **trust** animal behavior to predict weather. Mark an **N** where they should **not trust** animal behavior to predict weather.

2. After you finish reading, look at the places you marked with a **T** and an **N**. Use what you marked to help you write an answer to this focus question:

   Should meteorologists pay attention to animal behavior to help predict the weather? Why or why not?

   _____

   _____

   _____

3. Give two pieces of evidence to support your answer above.

   One piece of evidence that supports your answer:

   _____

   _____

   _____

   > Your evidence can be:
   > - A detail from the text, like a fact or a quote
   > - A detail from a photo, chart, or other text feature

   Another piece of evidence that supports your answer:

   _____

   _____

   _____

   > **CHECK YOUR PROGRESS** ☐
   > After you reread, make notes, and complete this page, check the box above. When it's time for the discussion, go to the next page.

WEATHER WATCHERS

Shared Inquiry Discussion

1 Use the answer and evidence you wrote on the previous page to participate in the Shared Inquiry discussion.

2 After discussion, think about whether your answer changed or stayed the same. Write it below. Then write a piece of evidence that changed or strengthened your answer.

Your answer to the focus question after discussion:

_____

_____

_____

_____

Evidence you found or that someone else used that helped you *(circle one)* **change your answer / make your first answer stronger:**

_____

_____

_____

_____

CHECK YOUR PROGRESS

After you finish this page, check the box above and go to the next page.

Unit 5   73

WEATHER WATCHERS

Essay Organizer

Write your answer to the essay question. Then write three pieces of evidence that support your answer.

Essay question: _____

_____

_____

Your answer:

Evidence #1:

Your evidence can be:
- A detail from the text, like a fact or a quote
- A detail from a photo, chart, or other text feature
- A fact about the topic, and where you learned it

How this evidence supports your answer:

74   Nonfiction Inquiry 3

WEATHER WATCHERS

Evidence #2:

How this evidence supports your answer:

Evidence #3:

How this evidence supports your answer:

Use these notes to write your essay. Then use the Writer's Checklist on page 131 to make sure your draft is ready to turn in.

WEATHER WATCHERS

Further Investigation

1. Look at the questions you wrote on sticky notes and the class list of questions. Think about questions that came up during your discussion, too. Are there any you still want to know more about?

2. Write your questions below, along with some ideas about how you might get started if you wanted to answer them. (For instance, you might look for an answer online, read a book on the topic, or ask an expert.)

Questions you still want answered:	How you might find an answer:

76 Nonfiction Inquiry 3

DON'T SWALLOW THAT SPIDER!

Prereading

In this unit, you'll read about urban legends, which are stories about weird or scary things that are not true but are still told over and over again. Before you read, answer the questions below.

What Do You Know?

What do you already know about urban legends?

_____
_____
_____
_____

What Do You Think?

Why do you think people sometimes believe stories about things that seem impossible?

_____
_____
_____
_____

Each time you read the text, return to what you wrote here to see if new information changes or adds to your answers.

CHECK YOUR PROGRESS
After you finish this page, check the box above and go to the next page.

First Reading 1: Instructions

1. As you read, mark a **?** wherever you are **confused or curious** about something.
2. After reading, look at the places you marked. Write your questions on sticky notes.
3. Choose two questions to bring to the sharing questions activity:
   - A question about a part that **confuses you the most**.
   - A question about a part that **interests you the most**.

Don't Swallow That Spider!

Jodi Libretti

The highlighted words will be important to know as you work on this unit.

Imagine you are at a sleepover with friends. The lights are out. Someone whispers, "Be sure to sleep with your mouth closed. The average person swallows eight spiders a year!"

"What? Really?" you say. You're **skeptical**.

"My friend told me. He knows a bug scientist."

"Well, okay . . . ," you say. You press your lips together. So do your friends.

Now, here's the question. Will you tell more friends about swallowing spiders? If you are like a lot of people, you will. This spider story has been retold and sent by email over and over. People all around the United States know it! But it's not true. Not at all. It's an urban legend.

skeptical: doubtful

Tales for Modern Folk

Urban legends are a kind of modern **folklore**. They tell about scary, strange, or weirdly funny events. These stories are often shared **orally**, in conversation. People also pass on urban legends through social media, like email and blogs. That makes them spread super fast!

The main idea of an urban legend stays the same every time it is told. But most tellers change or add small details as they pass the legend on. For example, the numbers of spiders in the spider-swallowing story might change. There can be many **versions** of one story.

folklore: stories that are not true, but that many people have heard or read
orally: using spoken words
versions: different descriptions or ways to tell about the same thing

> You've probably heard the rumor...
> While we sleep, we swallow as many as eight spiders per year.
> But it's **Not** true.
> That number is way off.
> Eight per year?
> Try eight per **night**.
> at least eight...
> Spiders love warm, moist places.
> They are in your mouth as you sleep.
> Dozens of spiders.
> Don't be misinformed.

Which details changed in this version of the spider-swallowing story?

Urban legends often come from "a friend of a friend." The events in them happen to regular people in the recent past. This makes them sound true. But are they?

Prove It!

Urban legends sometimes make people curious. They try to find evidence to prove or **disprove** them. The magazine *Scientific American* published an article to disprove, or **debunk**,

disprove, debunk: to show that something is wrong or not true

the spider-swallowing legend. It features an **arachnid** specialist named Rod Crawford.

Crawford says that most spiders are not interested in human mouths. They are busy tending their webs or hunting far from people. They're probably terrified of humans. Our heartbeat and breathing create **vibrations**. And vibrations mean danger to spiders. Crawford says he once heard of a spider being blown into a woman's mouth by the wind. But he has no proof of spiders *crawling* into human mouths. Legend debunked!

Many people are afraid of spiders, as this 1955 movie poster and the spider-swallowing story show.

Are Urban Legends *Ever* True?

Some urban legends do have a bit of truth in them. Have you heard the one about the candy that pops and fizzes on your tongue? People say that a boy ate six packs of Pop Rocks at a birthday party. Then he drank a can of soda and . . . kaboom! His stomach exploded!

So many people believed this legend that the candy company took action. It paid for

---

arachnid: an animal with eight legs and a body that has two parts (like a spider or a tick)
vibrations: small, fast, back-and-forth movements

newspaper ads explaining that there are tiny bubbles of gas in the candy. The gas is called carbon dioxide. It is also in soda pop. When the candy **dissolves**, the bubbles are set free. They pop, pop, pop! But there is only enough of this gas to make you burp.

Telling and Retelling

The spider and candy legends have been around for years. Why do people tell them even when they seem too weird to be true? People whose job it is to study urban legends have some ideas.

One idea is that people share urban legends because they're **entertaining**. Most urban legends are told in a **dramatic** way, especially the spooky ones. Just like roller coasters, scary can be fun! Mikel J. Koven studies urban legends. He says, "Life is so much more

---

dissolves: becomes a liquid
entertaining: fun and enjoyable
dramatic: with lots of feeling

interesting with monsters in it. It's the same with these legends. They're just good stories."

Others explain that people retell urban legends as warnings. Lots of people have fears about spiders or harmful foods. They often don't know the facts about these things. But they don't want to take chances. What if candy *could* make your stomach explode? People who repeat the legend think "Better safe than sorry!"

Finally, most people trust that urban legends are true. That's because the person sharing the legend is usually a friend. And urban legends are about everyday things, not dragons or aliens. It also turns out that people are more likely to believe an urban legend if it's written,

DON'T BE A BABY, NOAH. THAT STORY ABOUT ALLIGATORS IN THE SEWERS IS JUST AN URBAN MYTH.

I MEAN, LOOK BEHIND YOU... THAT'S CLEARLY A CROCODILE.

like an email. An oral story is not **permanent**, but a written story is. That makes it seem **official**.

But even newspapers and TV stations can be gullible. News reports once said that a woman was sealed to an airplane toilet seat when she flushed while sitting down. The airline said there was no proof of the event. What will people believe next? Did you know there are alligators living in New York City's sewers?

Quote in text is from "Urban Legends: How They Start and Why They Persist," livescience.com.

permanent: lasting or aiming to last forever
official: approved and allowed by a powerful group or person in charge
gullible: easy to fool or trick

First Reading 1

CHECK YOUR PROGRESS

After you mark the text with ?s, write your questions and choose two of them to bring to the sharing questions activity. Then check the box above and go to the next page.

DON'T SWALLOW THAT SPIDER!

Check Your Understanding — Instructions

- Read each question and the answer choices carefully.
- Look back at the text to answer the question.
- Fill in the circle next to the answer you choose.
- After you finish the quiz, turn to the next page.

1. Which of these things do all urban legends have in common?
   - Ⓐ They are proven false by scientists.
   - Ⓑ They are about animals some people are scared of.
   - Ⓒ They are not retold very often.
   - Ⓓ They are about weird or scary things happening to regular people.

2. What would a **gullible** person probably do after hearing the story about Pop Rocks and soda?
   - Ⓐ She would think that the story was not true.
   - Ⓑ She would dare someone to try the candy and soda together.
   - Ⓒ She would think that the story was true.
   - Ⓓ She would do research to learn about the candy company.

3. What is the main idea of the text?
   - Ⓐ Some news reports have said that certain urban legends are true.
   - Ⓑ Companies sometimes tell people not to be afraid of urban legends.
   - Ⓒ There are different ideas about why people tell urban legends.
   - Ⓓ People who retell urban legends often change details of the story.

4. Which detail from the text best supports your answer to question 3?
   - Ⓐ "But even newspapers and TV stations can be gullible." (p. 84)
   - Ⓑ "Others explain that people retell urban legends as warnings." (p. 83)
   - Ⓒ "But most tellers change or add small details as they pass the legend on." (p. 79)
   - Ⓓ "So many people believed this legend that the candy company took action." (p. 81)

DON'T SWALLOW THAT SPIDER!

Second Reading 2

1. Reread "Don't Swallow That Spider!" on pages 78–84. Mark an **R** where you see a **reason** why people might retell an urban legend.

2. After you finish reading, look at the places you marked with an **R**. Use what you marked to help you write an answer to this focus question:

   What do you think is the main reason people retell urban legends?

   _____

   _____

   _____

3. Give two pieces of evidence to support your answer above.

   One piece of evidence that supports your answer:

   _____

   _____

   _____

   Your evidence can be:
   - A detail from the text, like a fact or a quote
   - A detail from a photo, chart, or other text feature

   Another piece of evidence that supports your answer:

   _____

   _____

   _____

   CHECK YOUR PROGRESS ☐

   After you reread, make notes, and complete this page, check the box above. When it's time for the discussion, go to the next page.

86 Nonfiction Inquiry 3

DON'T SWALLOW THAT SPIDER!

Shared Inquiry Discussion

1 Use the answer and evidence you wrote on the previous page to participate in the Shared Inquiry discussion.

2 After discussion, think about whether your answer changed or stayed the same. Write it below. Then write a piece of evidence that changed or strengthened your answer.

Your answer to the focus question after discussion:

_____
_____
_____
_____

Evidence you found or that someone else used that helped you *(circle one)* **change your answer / make your first answer stronger:**

_____
_____
_____
_____

CHECK YOUR PROGRESS

After you finish this page, check the box above and go to the next page.

DON'T SWALLOW THAT SPIDER!

Essay Organizer

Write your answer to the essay question. Then write three pieces of evidence that support your answer.

Essay question: _____

_____

_____

Your answer:

Evidence #1:

How this evidence supports your answer:

Your evidence can be:
- A detail from the text, like a fact or a quote
- A detail from a photo, chart, or other text feature
- A fact about the topic, and where you learned it

DON'T SWALLOW THAT SPIDER!

Evidence #2:

How this evidence supports your answer:

Evidence #3:

How this evidence supports your answer:

> Use these notes to write your essay. Then use the Writer's Checklist on page 131 to make sure your draft is ready to turn in.

DON'T SWALLOW THAT SPIDER!

Further Investigation

1 Look at the questions you wrote on sticky notes and the class list of questions. Think about questions that came up during your discussion, too. Are there any you still want to know more about?

2 Write your questions below, along with some ideas about how you might get started if you wanted to answer them. (For instance, you might look for an answer online, read a book on the topic, or ask an expert.)

Questions you still want answered:	How you might find an answer:

CHILDREN OF THE OREGON TRAIL

Prereading

In this unit, you'll read about what life was like for children who traveled west on the Oregon Trail in the 1800s. Before you read, answer the questions below.

What Do You Know?

What do you already know about the Oregon Trail?

_____

_____

_____

What Do You Think?

Why do you think people traveled west even though it was a long, dangerous trip?

_____

_____

_____

Each time you read the text, return to what you wrote here to see if new information changes or adds to your answers.

CHECK YOUR PROGRESS
After you finish this page, check the box above and go to the next page.

First Reading 1: Instructions

1. As you read, mark a **?** wherever you are **confused or curious** about something.
2. After reading, look at the places you marked. Write your questions on sticky notes.
3. Choose two questions to bring to the sharing questions activity:
   - A question about a part that **confuses you the most**.
   - A question about a part that **interests you the most**.

Children of the Oregon Trail

Joyce McGreevy

> The **highlighted words** will be important to know as you work on this unit.

In the late 1830s in the United States, many people wanted a better life. Farmers had lost crops to floods. Deadly diseases spread through swampy river valleys. In some places, people of different religions did not get along. Lots of people longed for a fresh start.

In those days, a large part of northwestern North America was not part of the United States. It was a **vast** area called the Oregon Country. Native Americans lived there. Only some white explorers, fur traders, and **missionaries** had traveled that far west. The stories they shared

vast: very large in size or amount
missionaries: people who go to other countries to do religious work

Nonfiction Inquiry 3

This map shows what the United States looked like in the 1840s. The Oregon Country included what are now the states of Oregon, Washington, and Idaho, as well as parts of Montana and Wyoming.

tempted others to follow. They told of a gentle climate, rich soil, large forests, and rivers full of fish. Some called it heaven on earth.

A Land of Promise

The government began talking about giving white men and married couples free land in Oregon. Hope and excitement spread. People sold their belongings. They said tearful goodbyes to friends and family. Then they went to Independence, Missouri. That was where the Oregon Trail started. In Independence, families bought food and supplies to last five or six months. The trail stretched over 2,000 miles from Independence to the Willamette Valley in what is now Oregon.

tempted: wanting to do or to have something very much

Unit 7   93

Wagons were called "prairie schooners" because they looked like boats crossing the Great Plains.

In the spring of 1843, the first large group of pioneers set off in covered wagons for the long trip. There were about 875 men, women, and children and over 120 wagons! They were **emigrants** leaving their homeland for a new place. Other groups would make the same journey every spring through the 1860s.

Life on the Trail

What was it like to be a child in a wagon train, the long line of wagons that traveled together? Helen Stewart was eighteen during her family's **trek** in 1853. She wrote, "Oh it is beautiful," with "lots of cattle and wagons moving before and behind us and our selves moving on in the general **throng**."

---

emigrants: people who leave a place to live in another one
trek: a long, hard journey, often made on foot
throng: a large crowd of people or animals

The wagons were pulled by oxen or mules. They traveled only two to three miles per hour. A wagon train covered about 15 to 20 miles a day. That meant everyone woke up at 4:00 a.m. Children helped the women cook breakfast, clean dishes, and put away blankets. They also gathered up their family's farm animals. Men herded the oxen. At 7:00 a.m. the wagons started rolling.

Most wagons were about four feet wide and packed full of supplies. They had wooden wheels and no springs to soften the bumps in the trail. Most people, even children, found it easier to walk instead of riding in the wagon. Even so, the dust from the trail got in their eyes and made it hard to breathe.

So Much to Learn

Children could play and explore as they walked. They learned about buffalo, prairie dogs, and coyotes. They observed interesting landforms like Chimney Rock and Devil's Gate. They saw **geysers** and waterfalls. Many parents felt that the journey was their children's schooling.

Some families brought books and a slate. An older person would teach children lessons when they stopped for lunch or dinner. But most of all, children learned responsibility. Boys had to learn to hunt, drive wagons, and herd cattle. Girls usually cared for younger children and helped cook and sew. Some girls also rode horses and drove wagons.

Jesse A. Applegate was seven when he traveled on the Oregon Trail. He remembered competing with other kids to collect the most buffalo chips, or dried buffalo poop. Each evening when the wagons stopped, children had to find fuel for fire. There was not much **timber** on the Great Plains. But buffalo chips made the fire hot enough to cook meals.

Emigrants might have seen some of these animals along the Oregon Trail.

geysers: places in the earth where water naturally boils and shoots up in a spray of hot water and steam
timber: wood

Food and Free Time

Breakfast, lunch, and supper were usually the same: bread, beans, and bacon. One woman complained in her diary, "The only change from bread and bacon is to bacon and bread." Sometimes there was buffalo, antelope, or fish to eat. Most families brought along a milk cow.

After the evening meal, there was time to relax. Families often gathered around campfires to play music, sing, and tell stories. Children would play games like leap frog, London Bridge, and button-button. In nice weather, older children could sleep in the open under the stars.

Food Supplies for One Adult's Journey West

Flour	200 pounds
Pilot bread (hardtack)	30 pounds
Bacon	75 pounds
Rice	10 pounds
Coffee	5 pounds
Tea	2 pounds
Sugar	25 pounds
Dried beans	1/2 bushel
Dried fruit	1 bushel
Baking soda	2 pounds
Corn meal	1/2 bushel
Ground corn	1/2 bushel
Salt	10 pounds
Vinegar	Small keg

People used guidebooks to decide how much food to bring for their trip.

Dangers of the Trail

Along with fun and learning, there were serious dangers on the trail. Nearly one out of every ten emigrants died before the end of the trail. Many people died from accidental gunshots. Others, like Jesse Applegate's older brother, drowned while trying to cross a river. Adults and children were sometimes crushed by wagon wheels when they slipped or fell. But the biggest killer of all was sickness. With lots of people living close together, diseases spread quickly.

Unit 7

This photograph of an emigrant family was taken around 1870.

When the survivors reached the Willamette Valley, they were **exhausted**! But the work of building a home had just begun. Some would **claim** land and build their cabins right away. Others continued to live in their wagons or in shacks. Overall, about 300,000 people made the long journey on the Oregon Trail. Amazingly, about 40,000 of them were strong and adventurous children!

exhausted: very tired
claim: to say something belongs to you

First Reading 1

CHECK YOUR PROGRESS

After you mark the text with **?**s, write your questions and choose two of them to bring to the sharing questions activity. Then check the box above and go to the next page.

CHILDREN OF THE OREGON TRAIL

Check Your Understanding — Instructions

- Read each question and the answer choices carefully.
- Look back at the text to answer the question.
- Fill in the circle next to the answer you choose.
- After you finish the quiz, turn to the next page.

1. Which of these killed the most people on the Oregon Trail?
    - Ⓐ guns
    - Ⓑ drownings
    - Ⓒ diseases
    - Ⓓ wagon accidents

2. What would someone say to **claim** a lost book?
    - Ⓐ I lost my book.
    - Ⓑ That's my book.
    - Ⓒ I need to replace my book.
    - Ⓓ That is not my book.

3. What is the main idea of the text?
    - Ⓐ Many of the travelers on the Oregon Trail were children.
    - Ⓑ Travelers on the Oregon Trail had to eat the same food day after day.
    - Ⓒ Travelers on the Oregon Trail made fires with what they found on the way.
    - Ⓓ Some of the travelers on the Oregon Trail brought books and a slate.

4. Which detail from the text best supports your answer to question 3?
    - Ⓐ "An older person would teach children lessons when they stopped for lunch or dinner." (p. 96)
    - Ⓑ "Sometimes there was buffalo, antelope, or fish to eat." (p. 97)
    - Ⓒ "He remembered competing with other kids to collect the most buffalo chips, or dried buffalo poop." (p. 96)
    - Ⓓ "Amazingly, about 40,000 of them were strong and adventurous children!" (p. 98)

Unit 7   99

CHILDREN OF THE OREGON TRAIL

Second Reading 2

1. Reread "Children of the Oregon Trail" on pages 92–98. Mark a **G** where you see something **good** about traveling on the Oregon Trail. Mark a **B** where you see something **bad** about traveling on it.

2. After you finish reading, look at the places you marked with a **G** and a **B**. Use what you marked to help you write an answer to this focus question:

   Would you have wanted to travel on the Oregon Trail? Why or why not?

   _____

   _____

   _____

3. Give two pieces of evidence to support your answer above.

   One piece of evidence that supports your answer:

   _____

   _____

   _____

   Your evidence can be:
   - A detail from the text, like a fact or a quote
   - A detail from a photo, chart, or other text feature

   Another piece of evidence that supports your answer:

   _____

   _____

   _____

   CHECK YOUR PROGRESS
   After you reread, make notes, and complete this page, check the box above. When it's time for the discussion, go to the next page.

CHILDREN OF THE OREGON TRAIL

Shared Inquiry Discussion

1 Use the answer and evidence you wrote on the previous page to participate in the Shared Inquiry discussion.

2 After discussion, think about whether your answer changed or stayed the same. Write it below. Then write a piece of evidence that changed or strengthened your answer.

Your answer to the focus question after discussion:

_____

_____

_____

_____

Evidence you found or that someone else used that helped you *(circle one)* **change your answer / make your first answer stronger:**

_____

_____

_____

_____

CHECK YOUR PROGRESS

After you finish this page, check the box above and go to the next page.

CHILDREN OF THE OREGON TRAIL

Essay Organizer

Write your answer to the essay question. Then write three pieces of evidence that support your answer.

Essay question: _____

_____

_____

Your answer:

Evidence #1:

How this evidence supports your answer:

Your evidence can be:
- A detail from the text, like a fact or a quote
- A detail from a photo, chart, or other text feature
- A fact about the topic, and where you learned it

CHILDREN OF THE OREGON TRAIL

Evidence #2:

How this evidence supports your answer:

Evidence #3:

How this evidence supports your answer:

> Use these notes to write your essay. Then use the Writer's Checklist on page 131 to make sure your draft is ready to turn in.

CHILDREN OF THE OREGON TRAIL

Further Investigation

1 Look at the questions you wrote on sticky notes and the class list of questions. Think about questions that came up during your discussion, too. Are there any you still want to know more about?

2 Write your questions below, along with some ideas about how you might get started if you wanted to answer them. (For instance, you might look for an answer online, read a book on the topic, or ask an expert.)

Questions you still want answered:	How you might find an answer:

104   Nonfiction Inquiry 3

GRUNTS, FLOPS, AND DIVES!

Prereading

In this unit, you'll read about the ways athletes bend the rules to have a better chance of winning their games. Before you read, answer the questions below.

What Do You Know?

Have you ever done something sneaky to win a game or seen someone else do something sneaky? What was it?

_____
_____
_____
_____

What Do You Think?

Do you think it's okay to do sneaky or tricky things to win a game? Why or why not?

_____
_____
_____
_____

Each time you read the text, return to what you wrote here to see if new information changes or adds to your answers.

CHECK YOUR PROGRESS	☐
After you finish this page, check the box above and go to the next page.	

First Reading 1: Instructions

1. As you read, mark a **?** wherever you are **confused or curious** about something.
2. After reading, look at the places you marked. Write your questions on sticky notes.
3. Choose two questions to bring to the sharing questions activity:
   - A question about a part that **confuses you the most**.
   - A question about a part that **interests you the most**.

Grunts, Flops, and Dives!

Amanda Gebhardt

> The **highlighted words** will be important to know as you work on this unit.

Picture a school baseball field. The game is tied. There's excitement in the air. "Hey, batter, batter, batter. Swing, batter, batter, batter," one team chants. On the other team's bench, team members rattle the fence. Both sides cheer, yell, and wave their arms. They're rooting for their team members. But they're also trying to **distract** the other team, so they will make a mistake.

"It isn't whether you win or lose, but how you play the game." Grownups say that all the time. But winning sure can feel important when you're playing a game. It feels so important

distract: to cause someone to stop paying attention to one thing and start paying attention to another

106   Nonfiction Inquiry 3

that some players will do whatever it takes to win. Some of the things they do are perfectly fair. But others might not be.

Distracting or confusing the other team is an important **strategy** in many games. Football has trick plays. Baseball has change-up pitches. These strategies can fool the other team into thinking the players will do one thing with the ball when they really do something else.

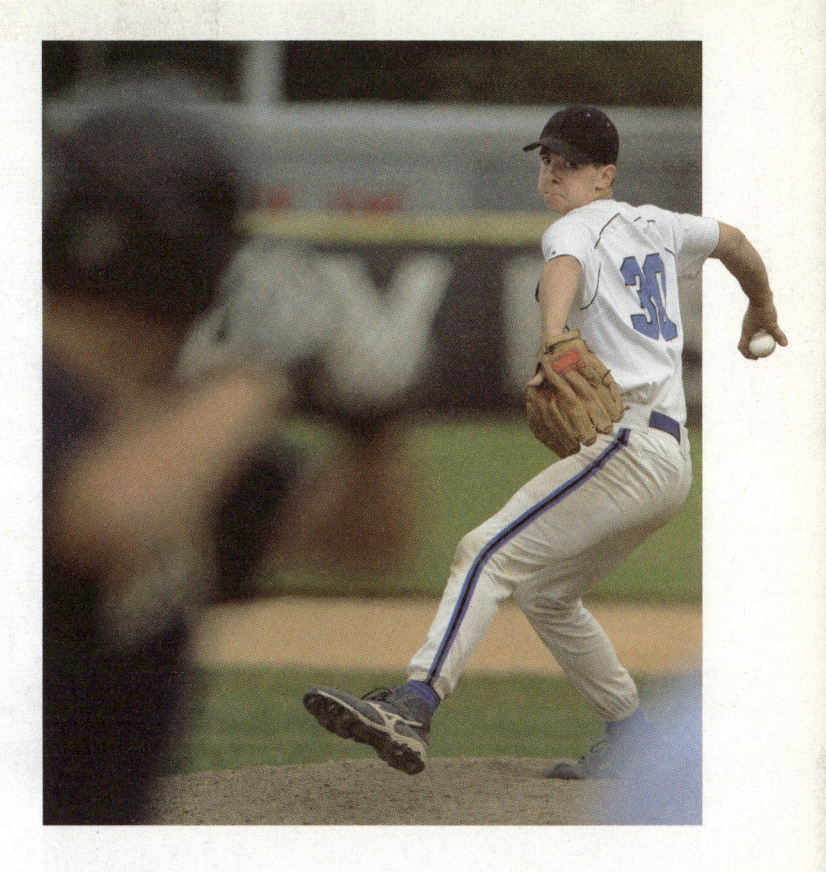

Sometimes players will bend the rules to get an **advantage**. They might make rude noises or even pretend to be hurt. But how far is too far? When is bending the rules a clever strategy, and when is it cheating?

Fair or Foul?

Rules are what we use to keep games fair. When one team breaks the rules, there are **penalties**. Often the other team is given a chance to score extra points. Basketball players get to make free throws. Soccer players get to take penalty kicks.

---

strategy: a careful plan made to meet a goal
advantage: something that helps make you better than others
penalties: punishments for breaking game rules

Unit 8   107

In basketball, touching another player is okay, but pushing is against the rules. What happens when players use the rules to their advantage? During a game, a player might fall to the floor when someone on the other team touches her.

"Ouch!" she yells as she falls down.

The **referee** blows his whistle. He decides the player was pushed and calls a **foul**. The fallen player's team gets two free throws!

But did she actually get pushed? Not really. The other player only touched her. Suddenly the same rule that was made to keep the game fair might now be used to score points. This trick is called "flopping" in basketball. In soccer, it's called "diving."

---

referee: a person who watches a game closely to make sure players follow the rules

foul: an action in a game or sport that breaks a rule

Many basketball players thought flopping was unfair. They said other players were trying to fool the referee. So now there is a rule against it. If a referee **suspects** a professional player has flopped, the player can be fined money.

Give Me a Break!

Pretending to be hurt or injured can get players more than an extra chance to score. It can also give their team a break. Many sports, such as football, have time-outs. These time-outs let players rest or think of new strategies. If a score is close, football players sometimes pretend to be injured to get their team an extra time-out. This gives them time to plan their next move.

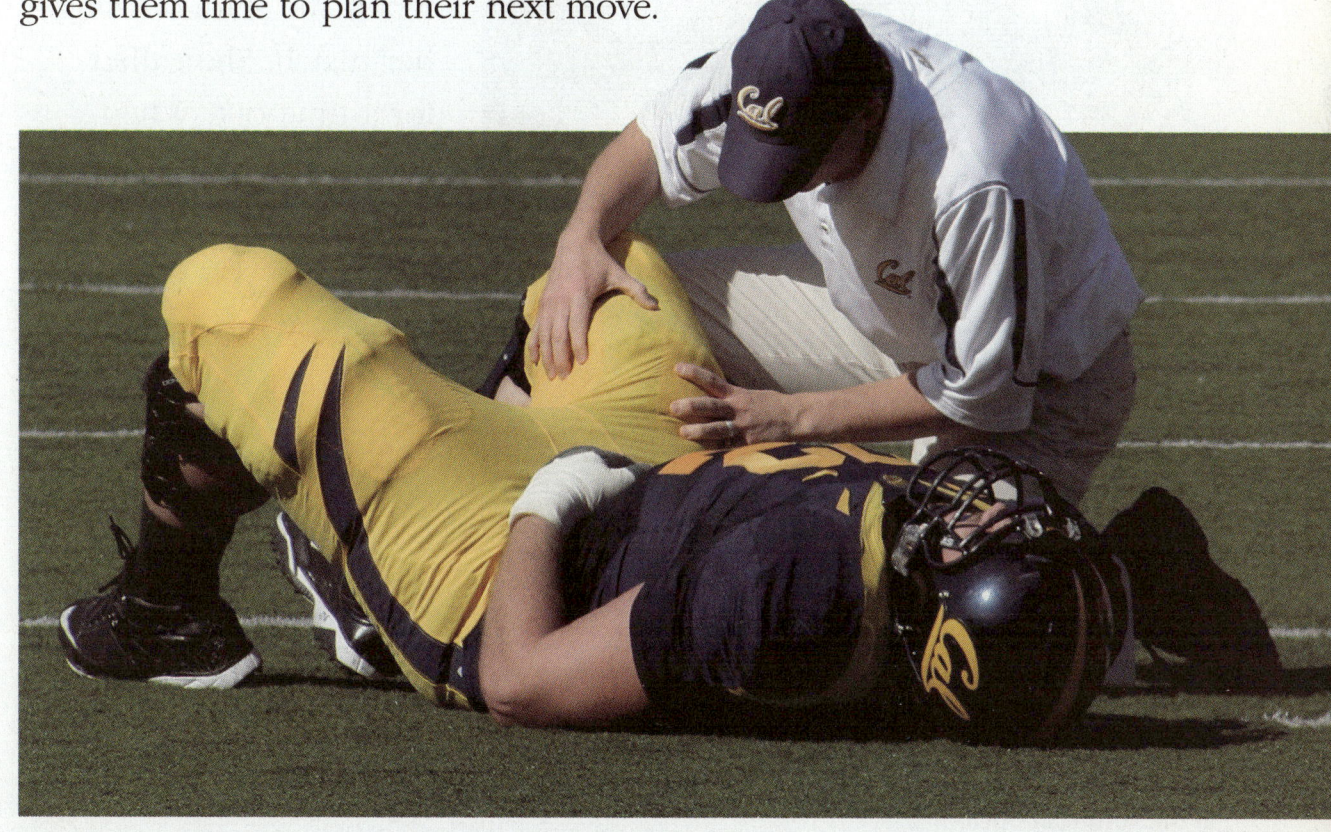

suspects: thinks someone has done something wrong

Some people think actions like that should be against the rules. But football player Martellus Bennett argues that it's all part of the game. "Every team does that," he says. "You've got to do whatever it takes to win the game."

Tennis players fake injuries to give themselves a break too. Some tennis matches go so fast that it becomes hard for players to keep up. Other matches can last hours. Having a moment to breathe can help a player stay **competitive**.

In 2013 many tennis fans thought Victoria Azarenka faked an injury when she started losing her match. She called for a time-out. When she returned, she started winning again. Fans were upset. She was even booed by the crowd during her next match.

Tennis players don't always pretend to be hurt to get an advantage. Sometimes they ask to go to the bathroom for a break. Other times they make loud noises.

After calling for a time-out at the Australian Open, Victoria Azarenka got to sit for ten minutes.

competitive: wanting to win and trying very hard to do so

110   Nonfiction Inquiry 3

Quiet Please!

Tennis is a pretty quiet game. The crowd only cheers after a player scores a point. Otherwise, it's silent. Except . . . what's that noise?

Maria Sharapova is a professional tennis player who is known for grunting during matches.

Some tennis players **grunt** when they hit the ball. Some coaches and scientists say that grunting helps players hit with more power. Others say it means the players are breathing correctly, which can help with their strength and balance.

But some players want the noise to stop. They say that grunting keeps an **opponent** from hearing when the ball hits the racket.

---

grunt: to make a low, deep, and short sound
opponent: the person or team one plays against in a game or contest

Unit 8   111

Tennis moves so fast that players need to hear the ball hit the racket to help them know where it is.

We all know that breaking the rules is cheating. But what if there isn't a rule against something? How can you tell what is or is not fair? The answer isn't easy. Sports reporters, coaches, players, and even fans all have different opinions. Until clear rules are set, players will have to decide for themselves what it means to play fair.

Quotes from Martellus Bennett come from "Martellus Bennett to Urlacher: All Teams Fake Injuries," nfl.com.

First Reading 1

CHECK YOUR PROGRESS

After you mark the text with **?**s, write your questions and choose two of them to bring to the sharing questions activity. Then check the box above and go to the next page.

GRUNTS, FLOPS, AND DIVES!

Check Your Understanding — Instructions

- Read each question and the answer choices carefully.
- Look back at the text to answer the question.
- Fill in the circle next to the answer you choose.
- After you finish the quiz, turn to the next page.

1. Which of these is the most likely reason a player would flop during a basketball game?
   - Ⓐ because she is hurt
   - Ⓑ to get a free throw for her team
   - Ⓒ to make fun of the referee
   - Ⓓ because she wants a break

2. Which of these things would you expect a **competitive** player to do?
   - Ⓐ work hard to win a game
   - Ⓑ be rude to the other team
   - Ⓒ get along with team members
   - Ⓓ be a good sport about losing

3. What is the main idea of the text?
   - Ⓐ Most sports games are won by teams who bend the rules.
   - Ⓑ It is hard to know when bending the rules is fair and when it is not.
   - Ⓒ It is hard to play an entire game without running out of energy.
   - Ⓓ Most players think that it is all right to do anything to win.

4. Which detail from the text best supports your answer to question 3?
   - Ⓐ "Pretending to be hurt, or injured, can get players more than an extra chance to score." (p. 109)
   - Ⓑ "But winning sure can feel important when you're playing a game." (p. 106)
   - Ⓒ "When is bending the rules a clever strategy, and when is it cheating?" (p. 107)
   - Ⓓ "Having a moment to breathe can help a player stay competitive." (p. 110)

Unit 8   113

GRUNTS, FLOPS, AND DIVES!

Second Reading 2

1. Reread "Grunts, Flops, and Dives!" on pages 106–112. Mark a **G** where you think a player uses a **good strategy**. Mark a **C** where you think a player is **cheating**.

2. After you finish reading, look at the places you marked with a **G** and a **C**. Use what you marked to help you write an answer to this focus question:

   Is it good strategy or cheating when players bend the rules?

   _____
   _____
   _____

3. Give two pieces of evidence to support your answer above.

   One piece of evidence that supports your answer:

   _____
   _____
   _____

   > Your evidence can be:
   > - A detail from the text, like a fact or a quote
   > - A detail from a photo, chart, or other text feature

   Another piece of evidence that supports your answer:

   _____
   _____
   _____

   > **CHECK YOUR PROGRESS** ☐
   > After you reread, make notes, and complete this page, check the box above. When it's time for the discussion, go to the next page.

Nonfiction Inquiry 3

GRUNTS, FLOPS, AND DIVES!

Shared Inquiry Discussion

1. Use the answer and evidence you wrote on the previous page to participate in the Shared Inquiry discussion.

2. After discussion, think about whether your answer changed or stayed the same. Write it below. Then write a piece of evidence that changed or strengthened your answer.

Your answer to the focus question after discussion:

_____
_____
_____
_____

Evidence you found or that someone else used that helped you *(circle one)* **change your answer / make your first answer stronger:**

_____
_____
_____
_____

CHECK YOUR PROGRESS

After you finish this page, check the box above and go to the next page.

Unit 8   115

GRUNTS, FLOPS, AND DIVES!

Essay Organizer

Write your answer to the essay question. Then write three pieces of evidence that support your answer.

Essay question: _____

_____

_____

Your answer:

Evidence #1:

Your evidence can be:
- A detail from the text, like a fact or a quote
- A detail from a photo, chart, or other text feature
- A fact about the topic, and where you learned it

How this evidence supports your answer:

GRUNTS, FLOPS, AND DIVES!

Evidence #2:

How this evidence supports your answer:

Evidence #3:

How this evidence supports your answer:

> Use these notes to write your essay. Then use the Writer's Checklist on page 131 to make sure your draft is ready to turn in.

GRUNTS, FLOPS, AND DIVES!

Further Investigation

1. Look at the questions you wrote on sticky notes and the class list of questions. Think about questions that came up during your discussion, too. Are there any you still want to know more about?

2. Write your questions below, along with some ideas about how you might get started if you wanted to answer them. (For instance, you might look for an answer online, read a book on the topic, or ask an expert.)

Questions you still want answered:	How you might find an answer:

BURGER WITH A SIDE OF SHOE POLISH

Prereading

In this unit, you'll read about why the food you see in advertisements may not be the real thing. Before you read, answer the questions below.

What Do You Know?

Think about a food you have eaten that looked different in real life than it did in an ad. What was different about it?

_____

_____

_____

_____

What Do You Think?

Why do you think the food in ads looks different from the food you really get?

_____

_____

_____

_____

Each time you read the text, return to what you wrote here to see if new information changes or adds to your answers.

CHECK YOUR PROGRESS

After you finish this page, check the box above and go to the next page.

Unit 9 119

First Reading 1: Instructions

1. As you read, mark a **?** wherever you are **confused or curious** about something.
2. After reading, look at the places you marked. Write your questions on sticky notes.
3. Choose two questions to bring to the sharing questions activity:
   - A question about a part that **confuses you the most**.
   - A question about a part that **interests you the most**.

Burger with a Side of Shoe Polish

Joyce McGreevy

> The **highlighted words** will be important to know as you work on this unit.

Do you ever look at an ad for a burger and suddenly feel hungry? In an instant, your brain notices each detail. See the grill marks on the juicy beef? Look at the shiny lettuce, pickles, and tomato. Even the bun looks perfect.

There's just one problem. Some of what you see may not be food at all. Unlike the burger that you order in a restaurant, the burger in the ad has hidden extras. These might include shoe polish, hairspray, cardboard, and glue. Welcome to the weird world of food styling!

When Playing with Food Pays

Your parents probably tell you not to play with your food. Guess what? Food stylists actually get paid to play with food! The job of a food stylist is to make the food in an ad look delicious.

So why not just plop food on a plate and take a picture? Food stylist Jon Davis explains, "We want your eyes to make your mouth water."

Making food look mouthwatering is big business. Every day **advertisers** wow us with online photos, roadside signs, and TV commercials. The images we see **affect** our eating habits in a powerful way. Americans eat out a lot. In fact, we spend billions of dollars every year on food we eat outside of the home.

All kinds of images compete for our attention. So food stylists use lots of tricks to make food appear as tasty as possible. For example, they might use shoe polish and a **blowtorch** to make a burger look grilled. They sometimes use toothpicks to hold lettuce in place. Some even hide cardboard between the layers of a burger. The cardboard keeps the food from getting soggy. Stylists have even glued seeds onto buns in neat, little rows. That can take all day. And you thought cleaning your room was boring!

advertisers: companies or people who try to make you pay attention to what they sell by making commercials and other kinds of ads

affect: to make a difference or a change in something

blowtorch: a tool that makes a very hot flame for melting or joining metal

Real ice cream melts too fast to photograph. But fake ice cream can be made from frosting or mashed potatoes.

What You See Is Not What You Get

Is food styling a creative way to sell food or an unfair trick?

Some stylists argue that tricks are necessary to show the food at its best. For example, stylists may brush household cleaner on the melted cheese in a burger. If they didn't, it would dry out and look yucky.

Other food stylists take a more natural approach. Some of them might not cook a burger all the way. This keeps the burger looking big and juicy. Even so, making food look good enough to eat often means making it **inedible**.

Some **consumers** complain that food styling is **deceptive**. This is a serious issue. It has gotten the attention of the Federal Trade Commission (FTC). The FTC makes sure that businesses follow certain laws when they sell things.

This food stylist is preparing a Thanksgiving meal for a photo shoot.

inedible: not safe or acceptable to eat
consumers: people who buy things
deceptive: made to seem true, even though it's untrue

122   Nonfiction Inquiry 3

According to these laws, advertisers must not **mislead** people about their **products**.

In 2008 one company said that kids who ate its cereal would pay attention better. There was just one problem. It wasn't true! The FTC ordered the company to stop advertising that false **claim**.

Which burger do you think was put together by a food stylist?

Is styling food the same as making a false claim about it? In 1968 an ad team was photographing vegetable soup. But there was a problem. The vegetables kept sinking to the bottom of the bowl. The team placed marbles in the bowl to push all the vegetables to the top. The advertisers thought this seemed like a clever and harmless solution. The FTC disagreed, and the soup makers found themselves **in hot water**!

mislead: to make someone believe something that is not true on purpose
products: things that are made or grown to be sold
claim: a statement saying that something is true
in hot water: an expression that means "in big trouble"

Unit 9 123

Food in Focus

The laws about food ads can be tricky. For example, companies can use fake food in an ad if the fake food is not the main product. So an ad for cornflakes must use real cereal, but the "milk" around it may be white glue. If the cereal sat in milk, it would get soggy. Besides, it seems that real milk just doesn't look milky enough!

Do you think this is milk or glue? What makes you think so?

So now that you know the truth, what do you think? Would you like to look at a picture that makes your mouth water? Or would you like advertisers to show you the food that you're really getting?

Quotes from Jon Davis come from "The Secrets of Food Photography," foxnews.com.

First Reading 1

CHECK YOUR PROGRESS

After you mark the text with ?s, write your questions and choose two of them to bring to the sharing questions activity. Then check the box above and go to the next page.

BURGER WITH A SIDE OF SHOE POLISH

Check Your Understanding

Instructions

- Read each question and the answer choices carefully.
- Look back at the text to answer the question.
- Fill in the circle next to the answer you choose.
- After you finish the quiz, turn to the next page.

1. What is the main job of a food stylist?
   - Ⓐ trying out new food
   - Ⓑ telling people about food
   - Ⓒ photographing the food in ads
   - Ⓓ making the food in ads look tasty

2. How might you feel if you thought a food ad was **deceptive**?
   - Ⓐ happy
   - Ⓑ angry
   - Ⓒ scared
   - Ⓓ excited

3. What is the main idea of the text?
   - Ⓐ Some food stylists do not change the way food looks.
   - Ⓑ Americans spend lots of money eating out every year.
   - Ⓒ Food stylists use tricks to make the food in ads look its best.
   - Ⓓ Food companies know that ads compete for our attention.

4. Which detail from the text best supports your answer to question 3?
   - Ⓐ "The laws about food ads can be tricky." (p. 124)
   - Ⓑ "The images we see affect our eating habits in a powerful way." (p. 121)
   - Ⓒ "In 2008 one company said that kids who ate their cereal would pay attention better." (p. 123)
   - Ⓓ "In fact, we spend billions of dollars every year on food we eat outside of the home." (p. 121)

BURGER WITH A SIDE OF SHOE POLISH

Second Reading 2

1. Reread "Burger with a Side of Shoe Polish" on pages 120–124. Mark an **F** where you see a **fair** reason to use food styling. Mark a **U** where you see an **unfair** reason to use food styling.

2. After you finish reading, look at the places you marked with an **F** and a **U**. Use what you marked to help you write an answer to this focus question:

   Do you think it is fair or unfair to use food styling in ads?

   _____
   _____
   _____

3. Give two pieces of evidence to support your answer above.

   One piece of evidence that supports your answer:

   _____
   _____
   _____

   Another piece of evidence that supports your answer:

   _____
   _____

   Your evidence can be:
   - A detail from the text, like a fact or a quote
   - A detail from a photo, chart, or other text feature

   CHECK YOUR PROGRESS ☐
   After you reread, make notes, and complete this page, check the box above. When it's time for the discussion, go to the next page.

126 Nonfiction Inquiry 3

BURGER WITH A SIDE OF SHOE POLISH

Shared Inquiry Discussion

1. Use the answer and evidence you wrote on the previous page to participate in the Shared Inquiry discussion.

2. After discussion, think about whether your answer changed or stayed the same. Write it below. Then write a piece of evidence that changed or strengthened your answer.

Your answer to the focus question after discussion:

_____

_____

_____

Evidence you found or that someone else used that helped you *(circle one)* **change your answer / make your first answer stronger:**

_____

_____

_____

CHECK YOUR PROGRESS

After you finish this page, check the box above and go to the next page.

Unit 9 127

BURGER WITH A SIDE OF SHOE POLISH

Essay Organizer

Write your answer to the essay question. Then write three pieces of evidence that support your answer.

Essay question: _____

_____

_____

Your answer:

Evidence #1:

Your evidence can be:
- A detail from the text, like a fact or a quote
- A detail from a photo, chart, or other text feature
- A fact about the topic, and where you learned it

How this evidence supports your answer:

128   Nonfiction Inquiry 3

BURGER WITH A SIDE OF SHOE POLISH

Evidence #2:

How this evidence supports your answer:

Evidence #3:

How this evidence supports your answer:

> Use these notes to write your essay. Then use the Writer's Checklist on page 131 to make sure your draft is ready to turn in.

Unit 9

BURGER WITH A SIDE OF SHOE POLISH

Further Investigation

1. Look at the questions you wrote on sticky notes and the class list of questions. Think about questions that came up during your discussion, too. Are there any you still want to know more about?

2. Write your questions below, along with some ideas about how you might get started if you wanted to answer them. (For instance, you might look for an answer online, read a book on the topic, or ask an expert.)

Questions you still want answered:	How you might find an answer:

WRITER'S CHECKLIST

Use this checklist to see if you have completed the important parts of your essay draft. If anything is missing, go back and revise your draft before you turn it in.

Does your draft include . . .

- ✓ a title?
- ✓ an introduction?
- ✓ a conclusion?

Did you . . .

- ✓ state the question?
- ✓ state your answer to the question?
- ✓ give three pieces of evidence that support your answer?
- ✓ explain how your evidence supports your answer?

Did you proofread your draft for . . .

- ✓ spelling?
- ✓ grammar?
- ✓ punctuation?

ACKNOWLEDGMENTS

All possible care has been taken to secure permission and provide appropriate credit for the photographic materials in this book. The publisher will correct any omission called to our attention in subsequent editions. The Great Books Foundation wishes to thank the following rights holders for permission to reprint copyrighted material.

Cover (clockwise from top left) © Paul J. Fusco/Science Source. Honda Asimo robot courtesy of American Honda Motor Co. © johnkp/iStockphoto.com.

1–2 © 2015 The Great Books Foundation. **3** © 2015 The Great Books Foundation. © Monkey Business Images/Shutterstock.com. **4–5** © GlobalStock/iStockphoto.com. © Susan Chiang/iStockphoto.com. © Marilyn Nieves/iStockphoto.com. © Steve Debenport/iStockphoto.com. © Susan Chiang/iStockphoto.com. **8–9** © Dario Lo Presti/Shutterstock.com. © Tatiana Shepeleva/Shutterstock.com. **10–11** Photo courtesy of Carnegie Mellon University. © Haruyoshi Yamaguchi/Corbis/AP Images. **12–13** Molly photo courtesy of Robosoft. Palro photo courtesy of Fujisoft. © Kyodo/AP Images. **14** © DM7/Shutterstock.com. **22–23** © Vaju Ariel/Shutterstock.com. "CI boardwalk Sandy sweepers" by Jim Henderson is licensed under CC0 1.0. Kymani photo courtesy of KQ Cares/Tania Dunbar. **24–25** Kymani photo courtesy of KQ Cares/Tania Dunbar. © Barabasa/Shutterstock.com. **26–27** Photos courtesy of Kathleen Carscadden. **28** © a katz/Shutterstock.com. **36–37** © Christoph Kakur/iStockphoto.com. © Tati Nova photo Mexico/Shutterstock.com. **38–39** © duncan1890/iStockphoto.com. © Aysezgicmeli/Shutterstock.com. **40–41** Photo courtesy of Francisco X. Alarcón. © frentusha/iStockphoto.com. **42** © wavebreakmedia/Shutterstock.com. **50–51** © Cheryl E. Davis/Shutterstock.com. © Cindy Underwood/Shutterstock.com. © Tim Ekkuitt/Shutterstock.com. © Pictureguy/Shutterstock.com. **52–53** © National Parks Singapore. © Eric Isselee/Shutterstock.com. © Gina Hendrick/Shutterstock.com. **54–55** © Steve Heap/Shutterstock.com. © NeonLight/Shutterstock.com. "Savannah Sparrow, Passerculus sandwichensis, nestlings and eggs with much larger Brown-headed cowbird, Molothrus ater, nestling" by Kati Fleming is licensed under CC BY 3.0. © Steve Byland/Shutterstock.com. **56** © Tim Hopwood. **64–65** © smebeesley/Shutterstock.com. © ZUMA Press, Inc./Alamy Stock Photo. **66–67** Photo courtesy of Brigham Young University. © Honza Krej/Shutterstock.com. **68–69** © David Rydevik. © konmesa/iStockphoto.com. © Phansak/Shutterstock.com. © LilKar/Shutterstock.com. **70** © Alex Valent/Shutterstock.com. **78–79** © Ernesto Victor Saul Herrera Hernandez/iStockphoto.com. © johnkp/iStockphoto.com. **80–81** Cartoon courtesy of www.edgarmcherly.com. © Pictorial Press Ltd/Alamy Stock Photo. **82–83** © 2015 Rachel Claff/The Great Books Foundation. © studiostoks/Shutterstock.com. **84** © www.cartoonstock.com. **92–93** © Everett Historical/Shutterstock.com. © Peter Bardocz/Shutterstock.com. © North Wind Picture Archives. **94–95** © Nancy Carter/North Wind Picture Archives. © North Wind Picture Archives. **96–97** Illustration from *Our Western Empire,* © 1881. © Anelina/Shutterstock.com **98** Peter Newark American Pictures/Bridgeman Images. **106–107** © makieni/Shutterstock.com. © Nagel Photography/Shutterstock.com. **108–109** © Aspen Photo/Shutterstock.com. "IMG_0700" by John Martinez Pavliga is licensed under CC BY 2.0. **110–111**. © AP Photo/Andrew Brownbill. "IMG_2758" by Marianne Bevis is licensed under CC BY-ND 2.0. **112** © Cynthia Farmer/Shutterstock.com. **120–121** © Christian Draghici/Shutterstock.com. © Laurin Rinder/Shutterstock.com. © BW Folsom/Shutterstock.com. © Eltoddo/iStockphoto.com. **122–123** © Cameron Whitman/Stocksy. Photo courtesy of Wendy's. Photo courtesy of Food Paparazzi. **124** © martiapunts/Shutterstock.com.

Design by THINK Book Works.